Don't Tell The Bumble Bee

By Jack Russell

PDC Inspiration
www.pdcinspiration.com

Illustrations by Neil Rogers (neil@felixe.globalnet.co.uk)
Typeset by WestKey Ltd
Printed and Bound by Rowe the Printers, Hayle

Many people end their lives with their music still in them.

This small book will help you find and play your own music.
For now is the time to grasp tomorrow.

The Author

Twenty years ago people laughed when Jack Russell told them he would become one of Britain's leading inspirational speakers and outdoor specialists. Well, they're not laughing now.

True to his word – and his self-belief – Jack Russell has become one of Britain's leading experts on the psychology of personal development working in both indoor and outdoor environments. During the last two decades he has been passionate about helping people develop their real potential and has explored what it is that motivates people and gives them confidence and self-belief. He has helped thousands to use positive communication and helped build dynamic and effective teams. Jack expertly combines his many outdoor qualifications with NLP Master Practitioner knowledge and a degree in psychology and recreation. He is a Level Five kayak coach, a sailor, kite surfer and much sought-after international expedition leader, who today lives in Devon.

The Author

Jack has worked with royalty, celebrities and top corporations such as the BBC, Bluestone, South West Water and Orange. He has inspired officers to develop the skills that will make them the leaders of tomorrow in both the Royal Navy and the Royal Marines. He has selected men and women to go to the North and South Poles. Through running leadership courses and personal development programmes, he has worked with thousands of young people to help them develop confidence and self belief. Jack believes so passionately that we do not put enough time into life skills in this country that he started a crusade in 2002 – running, walking, kayaking and cycling 1200 miles from Shetland to the Scilly Isles on an expedition called 'Journey to inspire our Nation'. Megaphone in hand he stopped in every town and city on route to give a motivational talk on education in Britain.

Jack practices what he preaches. He has skied to the North Pole, cycled over 12000 miles around the world, run four marathons, completed eight gruelling Devizes to Westminster kayak races paddling a total of 1000 racing miles, has been awarded a medal for personal courage and set up two successful businesses.

At the core of Jack's success lies a deep passion for people. It's a passion that bounces off the pages of this book as he shares with you seven fundamental skills that can change your life.

Tom Keene 2006
Author, broadcaster and sea kayak companion.

Contents

To Bee or Not to Bee   ix
Introduction   1

Chapter One   7
Spread Your Wings and Fly (Comfort Zones)

Chapter Two   25
Put Buzz in Your Life (Positive Focus)

Chapter Three   45
Buzz Words (Communication)

Chapter Four   69
Queen Bee (Personal Leadership)

Chapter Five   89
Make Honey (Relationships)

Chapter Six   105
Get the Pollen (Goals)

Chapter Seven   121
Sting in Your Tail (Motivation)

The Bee All and End All   139
Deep into the Blue   141
References and Further Reading   143

To Bee or Not To Bee

Spring 2006

"The Bumble Bees come alive and go to work to make honey – keep flying my friends"

Jack Russell

This book is dedicated to my parents whom I love massively. My father gave me a passion for adventure and the outdoors. My mother gave me the skills and passion for people. 'Thank you'.

I thought that I could write this book on my own. How wrong I was! The following people have inspired me to put my beliefs on paper. The work is not just my own but has been inspired by the following legends – Stephen Covey, Richard Bandler, Dr John Potter, Anthony Robbins, Zig Ziglar, Paul McKenna, Jack Black, Alan Pease, Tony Buzan, Daniel Goleman, and many more.

With very special thanks to:
Anna Thompson and Tom Keene for their help and support.

And also to my friends:
Nick and Helena Russell, David and Katharine Ewens, Sarah Widdon, Paul Turner (aka Bullet), Sara Gibbs, Rob and Debs Morris, Julia Martin, Jack, Izzy and Oscar Norris, Zoe York, Jane Morrison, Neil Lentern, Philippa and Nick Arding, Phil and Alex Way, Donna and James Timmis, Jane Gilpin, Liz Gartside, Peter Berry, Richard and Sarah Bury, Rob Pitt, Tom Inman, James and Anna Hastie, Charles and Yvonne O'Brien, Lucy Chappell, Fiona Guthrie, Kate Marsh, Natalie Dawkins, Annie Jenkin, Pat Coghill, Richard Ward, John and MC Ridgway, Iain Garland, Howard Marshall, Rebecca Seeley-Harris, Chris Wilson, Vanessa and Roger Ascough, Diana Young, Kathryn Blackie, Kate and Darryl Easton, Ella Reed, Mike Alderton, Pen and Mary Hadow, Andrew and Coralie Laurie, Mitch Bewsey, Andy Bradford and Gabrielle Cross, Mike Tomes, Steph and Eric Bridge, Paul and Emma Burchill, Chris Cook, Simon Westgarth, Louise Crichton, Gerri and Max Laithwaite, The Goddards, The Hawtreys, Chris Ingram, The Cables, JP Eatock, The Lawsons, Millie Coventry, Tracey Penna, Rupert and Tessa Hastie, Vernon and Helen Smith, The Hartleys, Kim Tucker, Penny O'Brien, The Critchleys, Clare Dyson and Terry Watts and to so many others to whom I am indebted.

Thank you also to all our special clients

Bluestone, Wates, Devon County Council, South West Water, Adventure International, RYLA (Rotary International), Eltham College, Strutt and Parker, Orange, Air Ambulance Devon and Cornwall, Kent County Council, Dartington Tech, Plymouth Albion RFC, RDA South West, Winifred Thomson, Michael Lloyd, All Women's North Pole Expedition, American Express, Association of Mountain Instructors, BBC Radio, Bond Pearce Solicitors, Calshot Activity Centre, College of Falmouth, Cornwall Enterprises, Denholm Industrial Services, Duke of Edinburgh Scheme, GMTV, NatWest/Royal Bank of Scotland, NHS, Nuffield Hospitals, Plymouth University, Royal Geographical Society Staff, Royal Navy and Royal Marines, Royalty, Sevenoaks School, The British Canoe Union, The Polar Travel Company, TMA Global, Tozers Solicitors, UK's National Outdoor Centres, West Country Ambulance Service, Wolferstans Solicitors, Cornwall County Council.

Introduction

Over there. Can you hear it? Over by the window, up against the glass. That fat buzzing thing, all noise and whirring wings: the bumble bee, trapped in a hot room on a sunny day.

You have, it seems to me, four options. You could ignore it, you could squish it (*why* would you do that?) or you could just open the window and watch Mr Bumble buzz away to freedom. That's three options. Option four? Step close, look at it. I mean it. Go on – really, *really* look at it.

OK – what do you see? You see tiny wings and a big fat body. No two ways about it – sleek, lightweight and streamlined *this busy guy ain't*. And, as scientists will tell you, Mr Bumble's weight to lift ratios are all wrong. There is just *no way*, say the scientists that, Mr Bumble Bee can fly (Antoine Magnan 1934[1]).

Except that, no-one has told Mr Bumble Bee.

And so he flies. (Now let him go.)

I believe very strongly that we all have the ability to do amazing things.

So… what often stops us?
    Other people's opinion that we can't, coupled to a lack of self-belief and self-confidence that gives room to a little voice, up there in our brains, that whispers "I can't. That I am unable, incapable, doomed to failure" (how I *hate* that word!).

It whispers we're not strong enough, not fast enough, not fit enough, not attractive enough. And you know what? If we listen to that little voice often enough, we start to believe it and get dragged down into the world of grey, gloomy-faced Eeyores to whom the glass of life is always not just half-empty but dirty, cracked and leaking, to boot. Been there. Done that.

But the Bumble Bee never told itself that it couldn't fly.

This book is about improving your life, making changes to the way you do things, the way you think, the way you regard yourself, the way you tackle the whole demanding, challenging, exciting business of living, *right now*. Life is a one-off.
Pause. Deep breath.
Think about that a moment.
This is it. No second chance, no dry run. Right now, your clock is ticking. You wouldn't expect a new car to run and run without fresh petrol, clean oil, a tyre pressure check, service or the occasional visit to the car wash, would you? Well, with my book you give the inner YOU an M.O.T. – a critical, constructive review of what you do and how you do it. It is a fun and enjoyable book that will allow you to see, feel, hear and think about things in a totally different way.

So hang on – your life could be about to change.

Do you remember learning about confidence, motivation, positive focus and leadership skills at school? Err.... Nope. Neither do I. Yet many job advertisements highlight these very skills as essential requirements. This book shows you a practical, simple way in which you can develop these skills – and there's not an algebra or geometry text book in sight.

When I was at school I found that life was pretty challenging and I was often put down – I wasn't just singing off the wrong hymn-sheet, I seemed to be in the wrong church with a different hymn book! Best days of your life? Not for me! When I left school I realised that in order to achieve what I wanted in life I was going to have to change the perspective I had been given by others whose motive, it seems to me, was to cram me into a suit of clothes that didn't fit. So I became my own private tutor. And, in that sense, my own best friend. I looked at the work of many great writers – Richard Bandler the creator of NLP; motivational gurus Steven Covey, Alan and Barbara Pease, Anthony Robins, Paul Mckenna, Jack Black and Tony Buzan who created mind mapping; Professor John Potter (a great mentor), Daniel Goleman, Zig Ziglar and his seminal work on goal-setting. For more inspiration I would recommend them all to you. I had, I believe, some other help too, for I really believe in the work of God. He has laid down valuable boundaries and codes of conduct, by which we can live our lives. [And, to those of you who flinch at that and think that I'm about to start off on some happy-clappy chorus of *Jesus Loves Me, This I know* – relax, I won't. But you should perhaps know that belief is something that helps *me*. Digression over.]

I combined this knowledge and a positive focus with my skills. When I taught geography and coached in the outdoors I helped youngsters overcome fear, build confidence and learn new skills. Sometimes, just watching the lights come on in their eyes after they had discovered the "CAN" rather than the "CAN'T" was reward enough. Perhaps it was there too that I discovered the depth of real potential that exists within *every single person* I encountered; all you had to do was drag it out into the sunlight, stand back and watch it grow.

However, I realised that you can have all the skills and knowledge in the world but without the correct attitude, nothing will change. The converse of that also holds true: <u>with</u> the right attitude you can do anything you want to.

I have developed my own attitude to life through the creation of positive experience and by stretching my comfort zones both

3

mentally and physically (more about comfort zones a little later). Put together, this knowledge, these skills and my positive attitude have enabled me to achieve many of my dreams. It is this that I use in my work, empowering people to achieve the seemingly impossible. It is this experience I want to share with you in this book.

Amazing Fact Number One: The conscious mind can only take in about 7 bits of information at any one time, plus or minus 2 (Miller 1956[2]). Later theories suggest it might be even less! Think about it: just seven bits of information. Based on that notion, I choose to focus on 7 key life skills and then break them down into 7 chapters, one for each day of the week.

Amazing Fact Number Two: Together these three 7's make 21, and it takes 21 days to change a positive or negative habit which is vital to personal success; it takes just 21 days to unlearn a bad habit, replace it with something good, wholesome and positive which builds up your own personal credit rating.

The information in these pages really **works**. I truly believe it is how to achieve what you want and to be happy. It is not a quick fix or easy to do because, just like turning flab into muscle or legs of jelly into legs of iron, we need to work at happiness and give it the attention it deserves.

The book falls into three parts. **Part One** looks at where you may be now and examines the possible reasons for being there. **Part Two** moves on to what you need to change to create the happiness you deserve and **Part Three** shows you how to maintain that change, not just for a day or a week or a few months but for a lifetime.

At a time when stress-related illness and mental health problems are on the increase, when obesity is becoming commonplace and the consumption of artificial stimulants is at its highest, I want to redress the balance and do away with the negatives that pull you down; change the way that you work, think and relate to others. I invite you, if you like, to download this information as *positive software* for your brain so that you can eradicate the negativity that has been around for too long.

Remember the bumble bee – it believes that it can, and therefore it <u>does</u>. If you told it that it couldn't fly, dragged out all the mathematical equations to *prove* that it couldn't fly, then it would probably shrug, fold up its wings and learn to walk.

Believe in yourself. Learn to fly. You are truly amazing.

CHAPTER ONE

Spread Your Wings and Fly

(Comfort Zones)

Inspiration!!

Thierry was a top French mountain guide. He had just reached the summit of his ice climb when he stepped onto a cornice of ice that collapsed – he fell 70 metres before he stopped........

I met him in Antigua as he sat in his wheelchair. I noticed the lack of push handles and an air of 'I can do anything'. I loved his huge smile and dry sense of humour.

Since his paralysing accident he has stretched his comfort zones and has just won bronze in the sailing Para Olympics.

He is an outstanding sailor, out on his own pushing the boundaries. I sailed past him – he was going solo on a Hobie cat (catamaran) with one hull in the water and one hull out. He had Velcro on his harness to stop him sliding off the boat.

I am passionate about kite surfing, and when Thierry saw the kite he confidently asked "How do I learn?" I asked if he would like to have a go; he responded in a wondrous French accent – "If you are proposing, I am accepting".

In turquoise water with the possible risk of tiger sharks it took three of us to get Thierry in the water and launch the kite. I stood on the bow of the boat with a 10m kite. Brendan (a headmaster) held the boat steady and Rob (a doctor) held Thierry upright in the water as his legs acted as a dead weight.

Three...two...one...release...up went the kite into the wind power zone and off went Thierry full speed and mostly <u>under</u> water!

To most people this episode would seem mad, but to Thierry it was mad not to have a go!

We picked him up after he had come to the surface and with the most monumental smile he raised his thumb in the air and shouted "Fantastique!"

What an inspiration to us all – often <u>we</u> are the only ones that hold us back.

We are all born with two natural fears – loud noises and falling. The rest of our fears become conditioned through life. So, what is it that makes us who we are? Why do we do what we do?

Is it the food we eat, potty training, the way we look, parental example, the way we brush our teeth in the morning? The answer is a little bit of all. According to Steven Covey[3] it's called – **determinism**. Determinism can be split into three parts:

1. **Genetic** determinism. This relates to the genes that we inherit from our parents and our grandparents and their grandparents and everyone before them. The genes we inherit determine how we look, our skin colour, eye colour, bone structure and predisposition to illness – our total given physical and mental make up. Sorry, but there's not a whole lot we can do about that. It's just the building blocks we were made with.
2. **Parental** determinism. This refers to how our parents treat us, particularly in early life. Hold a child's head under a running tap as punishment when he's small, chances are he'll grow up scared of water. How our parents behave towards us, their value systems, their beliefs, their sense of right and wrong – those are the attitudes we're likely to absorb while we're young.

   At an early, formative age when we're looking for life's way, parents are the ones with the signposts; it's their belief systems that often become our own. Later in life we can retain or discard those values as we choose, but at the outset those are the belief and value systems that guide us.
3. **Environmental** determinism. This is the most important area of our focus. Environmental determinism is all about who you choose to associate yourself with, who you choose to work with, who you have relationships with, your attitude and where you choose to live. It's about the choices you make about your surroundings. Environmental determinism is based on a single, simple idea: *That it is not what happens to you in life but what you choose to do with what happens to you* that is important. The choices and decisions we make in life determine who we become.

Environmental determinism encompasses the areas that become life-shapers and, thank goodness, it is these areas that we have the power to change. We can't change our genes and it is a challenge to go against our parents' values but we <u>can</u> manage our environment. We can choose how we live our lives, who we spend our time with and where that time is spent. Put the rest aside: in this category at least, you're in the driving seat.

So take the wheel and take charge: If you like your parents values and beliefs – great: Keep them, carry them on, bend them around your own lifestyle, but if you don't, you can choose to do things differently. It's your life, not theirs. Your life is to be lived on *your* terms, with *your* choices.

Comfort Zones

We all have our own routines and practices with which we feel comfortable and areas where we feel at ease. Collectively these are our comfort zones. When you have done something over 10,000 times it becomes 'hard wired' into your brain. It becomes intuitive, instinctive. Jack Black[4] put it so well when he gave the example of learning to walk – you fell over and you got up again countless times – there was probably never a doubt in your little mind that said "*Wow, if I get this wrong I'll be crawling for the rest of my life*". And look at you now: You're probably walking very well! You practised and practised until it became a skill that now you don't even have to think about.

Amazing Fact Number Three: There is evidence to show that the law of 10 enables people to become world class (Dr Istvan Balyi 2001[5]). If you do something ten-thousand times for ten-thousand hours and over ten years the chances are you will become a world champion. That means doing whatever you do well for two hours a day every day for ten years! If you developed the skills in this book for two hours a day for ten years imagine how you would bee!!

Comfort zones are created by doing things again and again and setting up a pattern or a habit that actually becomes easy and familiar to deal with; this can be a good habit or a bad habit.

Shrinking Zones

If somebody asks you to do something that is a little bit uncomfortable you can feel stretched, or challenged. It might be to stand up in front of a hundred people and talk to them, without notes, for five minutes. This may not stretch everyone, but for an appreciable number of others it would be the challenge of a lifetime. Just the thought of it brings some people close to panic. *"What me, stand up there? No way. I'd rather die."* And sometimes, they mean it.

If this has been the case in the past, if throughout our life whenever we've been challenged or stretched we've felt panic, had a bad experience, then, not unnaturally, our comfort zones

---

ACTIVITY BOX

Follow these instructions:

- Cross your arms
- Now cross your arms the other way

When we cross our arms automatically it feels very comfortable. You've done it thousands of times. In fact you've probably done it over 10,000 times. Yet when you try and cross them the other way it probably feels uncomfortable, you probably even have to look down to do it because it's not something that you have done over and over again.

---

become smaller. We become more timid. In a way, who can blame us? If it hurts every time you put your hand in the meat grinder, you soon stop! Exposed to bad experiences, those comfort zones of ours become like the little crisp packet you put under the grill: it shrinks and shrivels away to nothing. For many of us, when we started life our comfort zones were fairly large – the only fears we had, as I said, were of loud noises and falling. Then, through our parents, or through our environment, we *learnt* to be nervous and afraid.

This fear was not there to begin with; we became programmed by the negativity of others.

- *"Come away from the edge, you might fall."*
- *"Don't eat that, you might be sick."*
- *"Don't talk in public. You might get laughed at."*
- *"There is no way you can do that!"*

We listen to others' fears and heave them on board as unwanted baggage; baggage that, in future, will hold us back, stop us doing things we can do *if only we have the confidence to give it a go*. It is this transference of fear *from others to ourselves* that causes our own comfort zones to shrivel up and reduce in size.

Fear

If you look at fear and break down the letters, you can see the word as:

F – false
E – evidence
A – appearing
R – real

False Evidence Appearing Real. It is because the notion *appears* real that people start to believe their fears. The brain

14

doesn't know the difference between what the eyes see and the mind thinks. The thought of being on the edge of a cliff can be as frightening as standing on that cliff and looking down. Hence the reason you hide behind your cushion even though you know Jaws is not going to leap out of the screen at you (don't deny it we all do it!).

Time and again it has been proved: *do the thing you fear, and the death of that fear is certain.* Repeat it; believe it and it will become true: *Do the thing you fear and the death of that fear is certain.* Remember that fear, like the crisp packet, can be placed under the grill of examination so that it shrivels up and dies, becomes a discarded item of old baggage that is no longer of consequence. People have many fears – for some it is of failure, but for others it is a fear of being too successful, of setting yourself apart from others and attracting dislike because you are seen to be better/ different/ more successful than they are. It is easier to avoid what it is we fear than to face it, so we keep within our comfort zones where it is safe, cosy and protected. Yet in doing so we short-change ourselves and the fulfilment of our potential. The courage is there, within you, to take that first step forward. All you have to do is find it.

Easy Vs. Effort

Throughout history mankind has strived to make things more comfortable for himself. We started living a very primitive existence in caves, then moved on to develop the most luxurious of habitats and life-styles. Man has always struggled and fought to make his life more comfortable. As human beings we don't like to be uncomfortable, we don't like to sleep in an area where it is cold or damp or be uncomfortable due to lack of food, water or the occasional take-away or ice-cream cone.

Undeniably it feels good to be comfortable, yet too many people become too comfortable with the little they do. In a spoon-fed world where everything is within arms reach, so much is done for us that we have lost any sense of stepping out of our

15

comfort zones to do those things that really stretch and reward us. Most of us, given the choice, take the escalator instead of the stairs.

Does any of that ring bells with you? Where is your focus? Is it on ease or effort? Start putting more effort into what you do in your world, into how you work in your life and you can start to step out of your comfort zones and stretch yourself while making sure that you keep out of the panic zone.

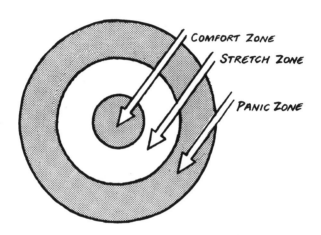

As a result of **Stretching** and **Stretching** yourself, your comfort zone becomes bigger as you do things which, just weeks ago, you would have thought impossible. Just as it's good to stretch your body, it's also good to stretch your mind.

The Mind

Our mind is almost schizophrenic; it has two parts to it, the **conscious** and the **subconscious** mind. A little like an iceberg the conscious mind is above the water while 80% of what is happening in our mind is below the surface in the subconscious.

Amazing Fact Number Four: The **conscious** mind is negative, critical, analytical. It's the one that talks to you. Your internal voice. It's your risk assessment centre, in the 'take care' mode. It only takes in 7 bits of information at any one time + or − 2. It is a little bit like the screens on a computer − if you fire too much information at the conscious mind it will overheat, crash, shut down and wander off for a large latte and a couple of chocolate biscuits.

Amazing Fact Number Five: The subconscious mind is in positive mode. This part of the mind takes in millions of bits of information at any one time. (Arntz W Chasse B 2004[6]) in fact about 2 million bits of sensory information enter the central nervous system and we process about two thousand of those every single second + or − 2! If you were to look at the subconscious mind it is often in the *'I can do mode';* it's in the 'take risks' mode.

The subconscious mind is the automatic pilot, the one that is opposite to the critical and analytical conscious mind. It's the one that automatically heals a cut and enables the body to function without the need for a conscious signal from the brain to tell the lungs to keep breathing or the heart to keep pumping. If therefore we could work more with the subconscious mind, if we could input more positive information into our subconscious mind rather than feed negative junk into the conscious mind, then we would be able to **Stretch** our comfort zones much more easily. Get the picture?

The subconscious mind has no filter. Think about what you put into your subconscious mind because it will come out in your behaviour (subconsciously) and your dreams.

With many people however, the **subconscious** mind is overridden and quietened by the **conscious** mind. The **conscious** mind tells us that we can't do this, we can't do that. It is a little bit like our defence mechanism, it's the one that safeguards us, it's the one that prevents us from stretching our comfort zones.

Often people drink alcohol or take drugs to quieten the conscious mind, so that they believe that they 'can do'. Sadly after too much they can't. Think subconscious.

The conscious mind is guilty of sabotaging many of us. It holds us back, keeps us overdue in the comfort zone saying "*Stay there, it's safe, it's easy. Reeeeelax. Take the easy option.*" And, meanwhile, the only life we have is slipping slowly through our fingers. A thought to share: One day, for sure, your life will be over. Will *your* song remain unsung? Will you be one of those whose greatest wish in old age is that you could go round again, take the risks, get it right, hit the high notes?

Think back to when you were a child at school and you knew the answer to the question being asked but didn't put your hand up – why not? A likely reason is that the chatterbox in your head was saying "*What happens if I'm wrong? I'll look silly. Play safe.*" It's that inner voice of insecurity. It keeps us in that safe zone where we work on very little of our true potential.

Amazing Fact Number Six: Scientists at the Stanford Institute for research in the USA found that most people only tap into 0.05% of their true potential. Zero point zero five percent! This is due to sabotage from the conscious mind, the critical analytical part of your brain. So thanks a whole big bunch, conscious brain!

Download Positives

To stretch your comfort zones focus on the links between your conscious and subconscious minds. Start allowing your subconscious to naturally take over and allow yourself and your conscious mind to talk in terms of **I Can....I Will....Do It!** Get your own back: start planting positive language via your conscious mind into your subconscious mind. By sending positive signals to your brain, the brain will process that information into your psychology and as a result your physiology will respond in a positive way. All you need to do is re-programme your automatic pilot and the job's done. Excellent!

Habits

By staying within our comfort zones we create habits. When you were at school did you ever score 20 out of 20 on a test, then find out that your peers had not scored so highly?

Did it feel uncomfortable to be too good? Because other people weren't up there with you, you learnt to play it down, sabotage yourself. Many of us have learnt through social interaction, by watching others, that to be too good is not a good thing. Such actions, if repeated, can become a habit – you avoid these successes because they make you uncomfortable. Often we set up these habits without realising it. When you do not believe you will achieve something you generally don't. You set yourself up for failure and in doing so you can create a lack of self-belief habit.

Negative patterns can lead to the following negative habits or addictions:

- A habit of no confidence
- Illness patterns
- A habit of saying *"I can't do this"*

Our belief systems are so powerful that as soon as we convince ourselves that something is right we start to do it over and over again until it becomes hard-wired. Neurological pathways are hammered down in the brain like rail tracks that say "That's how it is". For example – "I always leave it to the last minute", "I'm always late", "I'm no good at playing a musical instrument", "I'm no good at communicating with people", "I can't dance", "I can't........." etc etc. Heard this before? We get into the habit of expressing negative thoughts. But you <u>can</u> do those things that you deny yourself and, just by reading this, the process and possibility of change – from Can't to Can – has already begun.

Manage your Experiences

Positive experiences will help you to stretch your comfort zones. Take time to find people that make you feel <u>good</u>. Associate with the people that make you feel wonderful and disassociate yourself, or spend less time with, those who pull you down. Work out what it is that makes you feel absolutely *fantastic* and then repeat that pattern until it becomes a habit. Do it over and over again and go back to it. Ensure that the positive experiences in your life out-number those that you do not enjoy. Confidence is about positive experiences – it's about focusing on what you want, not what you don't want.

Are you truly happy with where you are and where, by choice, you have placed yourself? Confidence. Inner, deep-seated self-confidence; it enables you to stretch your comfort zones, while positive experiences outside those comfort zones boost your confidence. The two are inter-dependent. This is why we must choose our experiences carefully.

Focus on what you WANT

I used the word *choose* previously because life is about choices and we all have choices. We can either focus on what we DON'T want or what we DO want. Too many people worry about *"What happens if......"*, going over negative outcomes in their mind, and we know what negativity does to comfort zones, don't we!

Remember gloomy old Eeyore? *"It'll rain today. And if it doesn't rain today it'll rain tomorrow."* In fact, his week was blessed with endless sunshine, not that he noticed! In real life, whatever you believe tends to come true. Remember it takes about 10,000 times for a thought or a belief or an action to become hardwired into your brain. Going over and over negative thoughts in your mind will lead to fixed beliefs.

Beliefs start off as an opinion, they then become a belief and finally they become a conviction. We need to see ourselves in a positive way until it too becomes a conviction. **Use the mantra of the Lego super hero Jack Stone[7]: Can Do..... Will Do......Done!**

Amazing Fact Number Seven: Body language accounts for **55%** of your total communication. The words you use are empty if your body language is saying something else. So when you walk, when you talk, when you listen, when you eat, when you show love to others, do it in a way that makes you feel really, really confident.

Begin with your comfort zones. Where are you right now? Where do you want to get to and how will you get there? You have massive, massive banks of potential – explore them. We all have the same amount of hours in our day we just don't know how many days we have. Make sure you have no regrets. Play your music.

Do:
• Stretch your comfort zones.
• Surround yourself with people and experiences that make you feel confident.
• Replace ease with effort.
• Focus on what you want.
• Make 'Can Do' a way of life.

Remember:
Stepping out of your comfort zones is often *short term pain for long term gain*.

Stretch your comfort zones gradually so as not to enter the panic zone.

Notes

Notes

CHAPTER TWO

Put Buzz in Your Life

(Positive Focus)

Izzy and Effort!

Izzy is one of the most positive young people that I have ever met. At a young age she has learned to use the magic of emotional intelligence. Her eternal positive focus and enthusiasm for helping others has always amazed me.

Often adults think that they are teachers to the young, but we can learn much from young people. Their minds are clear from prejudice, jealousy, greed, anger and other emotions that can blur an adult's potential. Izzy would always point out life's good things and see the best in people and animals.

She is only 10 but in those 10 years she has learnt to deal with many of life's challenges – her father left home when she was 3 living far away in Hong Kong.

Izzy always has time for people and always wants to help – she will put others above herself. One such example is that she coached a friend around a cross country course, not interested in her own position, putting her friend before herself. Her positive attitude is that if you help others in their challenge you forget your own challenge.

A lesson Izzy taught me was effort Vs. ease. We were at Heathrow airport standing at the bottom of an escalator and flight of stairs. She looked at me and said "Shall we do 'easy' or 'effort'?" We chose 'effort' and walked the stairs!

Izzy counted the number of people on the escalator 'taking easy' and commented to me that if more people focused on being positive then that required effort. Although this itself does take effort the rewards are much higher than those reaped from taking 'easy'.

She is a young inspiration and positive role model in a world where people are opting for an easy life. I hope that she changes life rather than life changes her.

Think about this! Our brain is the most advanced computer known to man. A scientist once told me that if they tried to recreate just one human brain they would need to keep it in the Houses of Parliament and use the River Thames to cool it! It's a truly phenomenal piece of equipment. Imagine how much it would be worth on the open market!! Our brain is our onboard human computer and it weighs, on average, a surprisingly heavy three pounds – the same as a bag and a half of sugar!

It is divided into two hemispheres, the left and the right brain. Each hemisphere is responsible for different behavioural functions. The left side of the brain controls the right side of the body and the right side of the brain controls the left side of the body. For entertainment value we can split the brain into male and female with the right side being female and the left side being male:

ON BOARD COMPUTER

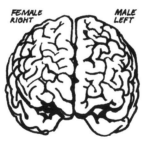

Colour	Logic
Visual	Lists
Awareness	
Intuition	Linear
Music	Words
Dimension	Numbers
Day dream	
Rhythm	Analysis
Creativity	Language

Everyone has the ability to use <u>both</u> parts of the brain, yet how much of each side of the brain we use depends on the amount of testosterone with which we were born. Testosterone does male things, mainly. If we have more testosterone we tend to use the left side of the brain. If we were issued with less by God's Quartermaster, then we tend to use the right side of the brain.

There is a bridge between the two sides of the brain. It's called the *corpus callosum* and it is the gateway, or link, between the two hemispheres. Sadly, in most men it is like a 1930's telephone exchange, which means that only small amounts of information can be passed slowly at any one time:

> *Right brain: "Hello, caller: you have a call coming in."*
> *Left brain: "Er.....Hold the line." Click, whirr......*
> *Right brain: "OK, OK, I'm holding."*
> *Left brain: "OK Caller, go ahead." Clunk, thunk and click.*
> *Whirrrrrrr and finally .....*
> *Right brain: "Left brain this is right brain..!"*

That's how things are with men. But with women, the connection tends to be as fast as one gigabyte broadband, and information can pass between the two hemispheres very quickly, hence the concept of multi-tasking. Our goal chaps? To use both parts of the brain equally.

The brain, or on-board computer, is so powerful that in an instant we can rewind and fast forward. Think back to the last time you were on a beach – there: you've done it – instantly. Now think forward to the next time you'll be on a beach and you've done that too – instantly. We can conjure up pictures, we can associate with images, we can disassociate with images. We can talk to ourselves, about ourselves, with ourselves. It's so powerful that the human brain can do all of these and more. Yet some scientists suggest that we only use 1–10% of our brain's total capacity at any one time. So why is it that up to 99% of our wonderful onboard computer just doesn't get invited to the party? It's a bit like using a computer keyboard and not knowing what all the F Buttons along the top can do. Our goal should be to start learning more about the function keys in the brain.

Our Psychology Determines Our Physiology

Just as you are what you eat, you become what you think.

We have to understand that what we put into this computer – our brain, our psychology – influences our behaviour and our state.

ACTIVITY BOX

Do this yourself or read it to a friend and get them to close their eyes.

Imagine a lemon; I'd like you to imagine slicing that lemon open. Seeing the shiny, watery sections inside. Smelling the aroma. Then think about biting deep into the bitter lemon. Allowing the juices to go to the back of your throat, stinging your lips. Notice the pith against your tongue and the bitter taste. Feel the segments against your tongue.

OK – you can now open your eyes.

Did you start to salivate? Did you taste that lemon? The fact was that there was <u>no lemon</u>. The reality was just words on a page that you put into your mind, or spoken words that you placed into another person's mind. It was put into your mind, your psychology; the brain processed that information, and as a result your physiology responded by salivating. This simple exercise demonstrates that what we put into our brain is so powerful that it has an effect on us. If we put rubbish in, we get rubbish out. If we put negative thoughts into our brains it will come out in our physiology.

31

ACTIVITY BOX

Do this exercise on someone who trusts you:

- Ask your participant to stand facing you with their legs a shoulder's-width apart.
- Ask them to put their entire centre of gravity up in their head.
- Now put your hands on their shoulders and gently push them to your right and then to your left. Notice they will feel fairly wobbly on their feet.
- Next, ask them to put their centre of gravity deep down into their feet. Once they have done this, repeat your pushing motion from side to side. Notice how you will find it harder to move them this time as you try to push them from right to left and left to right.
- Finally, ask them to put their centre of gravity right in their stomach. Notice now that, when you attempt to push them from side to side, they have become rock solid.

What you put into your psychology comes out in your physiology

---

React or Respond?

Unfortunately, many of us tend to put negative thoughts into our psychology. Our language is often very negative. We react to the world around us, we don't respond.

ACTIVITY BOX

Please read the words and letters in capitals out loud and then answer the question underneath.

- POTS, POTS, POTS, POTS.
  P, O, T, S. P, O, T, S.
  POTS, POTS, POTS.
  (louder!)
  POTS, P, O, T, S.
  POTS, P, O, T, S.

POTS

What do you do at a green light?
(Professor John Potter[8])

If you have just said "stop" to the question – and you almost certainly did – wrong! The answer is GO!

The fact is that your brain reacted just as many of us react to situations around us. The brain is wired to create assumptions using past experience and quick associations are made in our mind. This helps us to process information quickly and make fast decisions using comparisons of current situations with past experiences, all done in the blink of an eye. The flip side is that sometimes the brain can make the wrong assumption leading to the wrong reaction for that situation – as with the above example. In our everyday lives it is good to step back from the reactions we feel (created from parent, environment and gene determinism) and look at the alternatives. It is so easy to follow these assumptions and habits that seem to work most of the time that we do not stop, step back and really scrutinise what we do. A strong example of this is the language we use in social interaction.

As a greeting we tend to ask people; *"How are you?"* and they will reply *"I'm fine"*. What........just fine? If you break down the word fine, to me it represents a:

- **F**eeling
- **I**nwardly
- **N**egative
- **E**xpression.

Or as a nurse once told me it could mean Feeling Insecure Neurotic and Emotional!! People may also say things like *"I'm not too bad"*, or *"Can't complain"*. What the brain reacts to is the last thing it hears – in this case 'bad' and 'complain'. So they are bad but they are not *that* bad, they can't complain – but they would like to! Another favourite is *"It's not a problem"*.

Ah! I see. I think. So..er...it IS a problem, but not that much of a problem, is that it?

Notice what we do: we respond to the last thing we hear. So make sure the last thing you and others hear is positive. I am 'great', 'fantastic', 'excellent'. Or how about: "I am, in fact, teetering upon the very brink of perfection." Yeah, that should about do it.

ACTIVITY BOX

Ask someone who trusts you to help you

- Ask your participant to put their strongest arm out in front of them. Straight out with their fist clenched and knuckles facing upwards.
- You are now going to attempt to push their arm down with your index finger, just one finger. Their arm against your finger.
- As you push down they are to resist and push up, but as they do this they are to say "I am strong, I am strong, I am strong", over and over.
- Repeat the exercise but this time ask them to try and resist you; the word try is a pretty weak word. ['Try', to me, suggests you are preconditioned to failure.] They must try and resist you but as they do I would like you to ask them to repeat the words "I am weak and negative, I am weak and negative", out loud.
- Just put the same amount of pressure on their arm with your index finger and see the result. As they say "I am weak and negative" you will find it easier to push their arm down.

Create a Mind Filter

With all this negativity around we need a positive strategy. Our subconscious mind has no filter on it. As it is processed by the brain, our physiology will respond. Think about our verbal language. We use words like *"I am tired"*. Which actually means you are telling yourself to <u>be</u> tired, rather than saying *"I could have more energy"*.

Another example: When we cannot remember something we say *"I forget"*, which actually tells the brain to forget, rather than *"I'll remember later"*. We say *"Sorry I am late"*, implying that we are inefficient. Surely it is better to say *"I'm sorry I'm behind schedule"*, implying that you've got a schedule!

We have a habit of using language that puts doubt in peoples' minds. For example, we will say *"Don't slip"*. Every time we hear the term *"don't"* we have to think about what the person is referring to before we think about not doing it.

Let me show you how this works:
Whatever you do, **don't** think about a pink polar bear sitting on an exercise bike.

Guess what? You are probably thinking about it right now! In the same way that a child jumps up onto a wall and says *"Mum look at me"* and the mum turns, gasps and warns *"Whatever you do, don't fall"*. Don't fall? The last thing the child hears is "fall". They must process what it would be like to fall, just as you had to process the polar bear, before they can process not doing it or thinking about it. By bringing the idea of falling to the attention of the child's conscious mind it becomes more of a possibility. Falling then becomes a self-fulfilling prophecy. I seriously doubt whether falling would have even entered the child's mind without that cry from an over-anxious parent.

Remember that the last thing the brain hears is the first thing it responds to.

Positive Language

95% of people are using negatives – so be a bit different: put in a positive or two. These negatives are going into our minds over and over again. Think about what you put into your mind, and think even more about what you put into the minds of others through the words that you use. Listen critically to what people say and notice how they say it. Then reframe it and change it into positive language. The most important message to get your head around is this: *as soon as we change our language we start to change our physiology.*

Tell people that they can, they will, they are going to and they are more than half way there. The most important words to replace are Can't and Don't. Put into peoples' minds the fact that they have amazing capabilities and the capacity to do anything that they know, deep down, they physically, emotionally, spiritually and mentally **CAN** do. This can open the gates to amazing opportunities, not just in your life but in the lives of those who surround you. Spread the word: think and say positive.

Make Positive Habits

Remember it takes just 21 days to change the habit of a lifetime. So now you can make a positive language habit. Notice people saying *fine, not too bad, not a problem, I can't, I won't, I'm unable*. As soon as you hear people, or see people, or even *feel* people saying these things, bring it to your conscious attention. Bring it from the subconscious recesses of your mind to the surface and make yourself aware of how many times you're hearing it, feeling it, seeing it. Take 21 days to notice your own language and turn it round into positive, powerful, enabling thinking. Attitudes, both negative and positive, can be contagious. Like courage.

There is nothing more contagious than enthusiasm, save the lack of it.

Contagious Energy

ACTIVITY BOX

Do this with others around you.

Make yourself yawn. Go on. Give a really deep, long yawn.
Notice how quickly those around you yawn too.
See how contagious your behaviour can be.

Now do the same with a smile. Start a conversation with a massive smile and see how,...almost inevitably, the other person smiles back.

We all know that there are people who will walk into a room and light the place up – your immediate reaction is "Thank goodness they are here". Then, there are other people who will walk into the same room and they will almost act as "mood hoovers", or "energy thieves". They will drain you, suck out the energy, and make you feel down and uneasy. Which sort of person are you?

A smile is just as contagious as a yawn. So why not spread one of those instead? Attitudes, as I've said, are contagious. And they can spread; thanks to you, to people you haven't even met. Here's what I mean: Imagine driving to work one morning. You're thinking about what to cook for supper tonight, what kind of mood your boss will be in and so on. The net result of all this inattention is that your driving is a little..er..shall we say sloppy? Result? You cut someone up, ruin their early morning mood of boundless optimism. Looks are exchanged – perhaps even a gesture or two. You drive away, they to their work, you to yours. Now that person goes to work with ten other people. They walk into work, slam their bag on the desk and spread the news: I Am Having A Really Bad Day. Those ten people are upset by that one person <u>you</u> upset. Now they go off to meetings and each sees *another* ten people. The mood spreads until, without realising it, your little bit of carelessness has upset about 100 people!

That said, there are four types of people that we need to look at:

1. People who say "I'm good and you're good", people who really get on in life: great people to have around.
2. People who say "I'm good but you are not so good", the people who put others down. The saboteurs.
3. People who say "I'm not so good and you are not so good either". These are people who could be more positive! They tend to associate with people who make them feel negative or tell them that they are negative. Mood hoovers!
4. Finally, you've got the people who say "I'm not good, but you're really good, it's always alright for <u>you</u>". Uugh! Eeyore's people!

Right now you are probably thinking *"Which am I?"*, *"How am I seen by others?"* *"What kind of mood or state do I create around me?"* If others had to select the last person on earth they'd choose to be trapped with in a lift, would you come top of their list? Near the top?

Do you add to the weight of smiles in a room? Or do you bring in the dark grey clouds of 'Can't do', gnawing self-doubt and gloomy depression? Think about it.

Wouldn't it be great if there could be more people who could say *"I'm great and you're great"* Be happy with yourself, be positive and give others the support they need to be happy. Smile. It's infectious. So spread it.

The Law of the Boomerang

Positivity has many benefits, the main one being that what you throw out you get back. The signals we give out are very important. I have great belief in the law of the boomerang: if you give out positive vibes then, chances are, you'll get positive vibes back in return. The converse is also true: if you give out negatives then you will get back negatives in return.

In some eastern cultures it's called Karma, what you put out you ultimately get back.

So how <u>do</u> you make yourself feel more positive? Easier said than done, you think. Not so, say I. Not if you follow these simple steps:

- Focus on the positive in all situations.
- Focus on what you want rather than on what you don't want.
- Focus on who you want to become rather than who you would <u>not</u> like to become.
- Focus on the people who make you feel good, and on the things that make you feel good.

Simply move away from those people and things that don't make you feel great.

We are surrounded by negativity; through television soaps and through news and 'car crash' TV programmes that put people down. These programmes consume and then discard people; they make a cottage industry out of suffering, failure and humiliation. Crime and violence on television has risen and this too has a subconscious effect. We listen to the news and read newspapers with images and words of horror, devastation and sadness. A bundle of laughs it ain't. Now, I'm not saying for one moment that we should avoid what is going on in the world, but I AM saying that we should put a limit on how much of the negative we allow to be downloaded into our brains, those fantastic onboard computers of ours.

Amazing Fact Number Eight: During the Korean war prisoners in the Korean prisoner of war camps were subjected to negative mental experiences which led to more deaths than those in the camps where physical torture was rife (Dr William E Mayer 2004[9])

So be around the people and the things that make you feel good. In the midst of all the dross and fear, life is also full of heroism, kindness and laughter. It's there – really. All you have to do is open your eyes.

Be Good to Yourself

To feel happier, focus on *you*. Get a natural boost by looking after yourself. Looking after yourself automatically makes you feel good. People always say exercise regularly and eat healthily – because it <u>works</u>! Eat less, move more!! The effects are phenomenal; exercise releases endorphins into the blood which are pumped around the body giving you a natural high. It also increases the oxygen to the brain enabling the body to become more efficient in body repair and maintenance, while increasing your thinking capacity.

Amazing Fact Number Nine: At the time of writing this book statistics show that 66% of adults are now overweight or obese in the UK (BBC health website 2006[10]). This has serious health implications for the future. Some of the major causes are high levels of sugar, salt, fat and alcohol.

In the past the amount of money you had tended to match your size. Being large was a sign of affluence. Now the roles have turned and today we see those with less money carrying the excess weight. A generalisation I know, but take a look around. Our world has seen several revolutions (get it?) the Agrarian, the Industrial, the Technological and in the future it is predicted that it will be the Psychozoic age.

Paul Zane Pilzer[11], a world class government advisor, explains that this will focus on the health and wellness industry. If current trends continue it is estimated that by 2010 we will have caught up with the USA and their obesity levels.

Make sure – starting now – that you're not one of them. Don't just talk about getting fit and healthy, <u>do it</u> now. Start today.

And, while you're about it, be encouraging when you talk to yourself. Put yourself up – make sure you constantly talk in positive terms. Tell yourself:

- I am doing really well
- I look fantastic
- I feel brilliant
- I am really proud of the way I handled that
- I can do anything I want
- Give yourself 7 positives to every 1 negative. The more you do this the more success and positive thinking will become hard-wired into your brain.

Make Others Feel Good.

In my experience people give on average seven bits of negative to every one bit of positive. We are all conditioned to say what did not go well rather than what went well. Hang wallpaper on a wall and sure as shootin' you'll show friends the bit you botched rather than the bit that went up without any problem.

Everyone needs a bit of support, a bit of encouragement. So my second way to feel positive about yourself is to make *other people* feel good in whatever way you can. Make a habit of complimenting others. If you can find time to seek out the little things in others that make them feel good, it can make a big difference. Provide them with the support they need to build their self-confidence and self-belief. Example? Well, how about this: When putting a child to bed ask them to think of one thing from the day they are really proud of, or one thing that made them feel happy. Close each day with a positive. Or, during the working week set yourself the target of publicly praising two people. This does take practice but you will soon find it easier to notice all the positive elements that surround you. Learn to give yourself to others.

Make a conscious effort to add something positive to people. Add something positive to their day and, who knows? They may add something positive to yours.

Remember that once you are convinced you are a positive person who looks good and feels great, everyone around you becomes convinced as well. When people are passionate about what they do and how they do it, other people become passionate about them.

Do:
- Spend time with people who make you feel good.
- End each day with a positive thought.
- Speak positively to yourself.
- Take regular exercise.
- Cut down on salt, fat, sugar and caffeine.
- Hydrate the brain; drink plenty of water.

Remember:

What we put into our psychology comes out in our physiology.

The law of the boomerang – what you put out, you get back.

Attitudes are contagious.

POSITIVITY TEST

Reframe these common phrases into positives, the first one provides an example:

I forget   *I will remember later*

1. I'm not too bad
2. I'm cold
3. I'm so tired
4. Sorry, I'm late
5. I'm fine
6. Take care
7. It's not a problem
8. It's not far
9. I won't let you down

Notes

Notes

CHAPTER THREE

Buzz Words

(Communication)

Powerful Communication!

Some say Nick, 36 years old, has the gift of the gab. He works in London in the advertising business. Most days he goes to work in a suit, commuting like thousands of others, day in day out.

His difference lies in his other work and passion. Once a year he goes to Africa, and stands up in front of hundreds of African church leaders where he communicates on a spiritual level. He is one of the most inspirational speakers I have ever heard. His message is clear – to teach people to tap into the power of God, to enable them to help and inspire each other. He talks of the need to be into humility from the word humus – earth – a sense of being grounded. His words, intonation, and actions are from the heart, fuelled by the power of his spiritual belief. His main message is that man is wrong if he thinks he can do it all without God or a spiritual dimension in their life. When he talks he uses a cool head and warm heart. I love the fact that his faith gives him such inner peace and love for others in a world of fear, fighting and suffering. I wish him every success as he and his wife Helena, a doctor, take a leap of faith and move to Uganda in 2006 – may the spiritual dimension of his life grow further as they give of themselves and communicate their love and care for those less fortunate.

www.

Three little letters. Insignificant, really.

Yet they've changed the world. They've rebuilt lives, made relationships, provided that Eureka! moment for millions and opened doors to a mountain of knowledge; they've built bridges to understanding, saved lives, and helped to plan perfect crimes and robberies we've yet to discover.

The World Wide Web has had a massive effect in terms of communication. We live in a world of modern technology where we can send an e-mail at 3000 miles a bloomin' *second*! We live in a world where we can all be in almost constant communication via mobile or satellite phone: Generals in safe, distant Washington DC can field-manage the assault of their troops in real time half a world away. At the press of a button we can text somebody, send out messages in an instant. Yet …yet with all this modern technology, how many of us have actually lost our ability to communicate with ourselves – and with others? If the answer to that is 'most of us', then what is the price of that progress?

We have, enlightened reader, two forms of communication. The first is *intra*-personal. That is, how we communicate *with ourselves*. It's what we think, what we say to ourselves; what we feel. It's the communication that goes on internally, how we see the world around us.

The second form of communication is *inter*-personal, the way we interact with other people and the environment around us. It's my belief that, with the wonders of modern technology, a lot of us have opted for 'Easy' rather than 'Effort' when it comes to communicating with others: It's very easy to communicate using modern technology. But to communicate effectively takes effort. Texts and emails don't come with body language attached, all the more reason to think carefully about the words we use. Before you fire off your next text or email, ask yourself is that electronic journey really necessary?

See, Hear, Feel, Think

There is a law called the Law of Use. Use it or lose it. Why don't penguins fly? Why doesn't man walk on all fours? (A few friends of mine still do, given the right circumstances!)

Because, at least in part, the need to do so has been usurped by what we like to think of as progress. In our modern electronic age one could argue that, because of emails and text messages, we have started to lose the art of communication. Put another way, we use communication indiscriminately. Many of us talk about having 'common sense' – yet, all that common sense is, is "What is common to me making sense". Hence using two or more of the following senses on a regular basis becomes common to us: visual (seeing), auditory (hearing), kinaesthetic (feeling), olfactory (smelling) gustatory (tasting) or our sixth sense – intuition (instinctively knowing). The majority of us use our visual, auditory and kinaesthetic senses in communication and most of us have a natural preference for one sense over another. If we listen to the way people speak, we notice that they will literally express how they like to communicate with the words they use. For example people with a **visual** preference (visuals) will say:

- *"I am looking forward to seeing you"*
- *"I see what you mean"*
- *"Looks good"*
- *"Picture this"*
- *"See you later"*

The underlined words are all visual. 'Visual' people need to be shown things, they need to see things, they need to be able to picture what it is you are communicating and have a vision of what they are doing. This all comes out through their language.

Auditory people love to **hear** things. They will use language such as:

- *"Sounds good"*
- *"I hear where you are coming from"*
- *"Good to hear from you"*
- *"I am all ears"*
- *"Can everyone listen in?"*

They are the people who enjoy listening to the radio, listening to talks or music. They will enjoy communicating on the telephone where they have to listen intently, and will often be very good counsellors and musicians.

Kinaesthetic people, like to **'do'** things, they say:

- *"I am hands on"*
- *"Let me get a grip", "a grasp", "a handle"*
- *"My gut reaction is"*
- *"The way I feel is"*

They will use kinaesthetic language because they like to communicate by doing. If you show them something they will need to touch it. They need to feel, they need to act.

We need to be aware of the way individuals take in information. Their sensory preference will determine how best they communicate and educate themselves. If an **auditory** person talks to a **visual** and asks *"Do you hear where I am coming from?"*, *"Do you like the sound of that?"* the **visual** will reply *"Well, it looks good"* and *"I can see where you are coming from"*. Subconsciously the **visual** may feel that they do not completely connect with what the **auditory** person is proposing because they are essentially speaking two different languages. But what if, with just a little thought, things were to change? What if the **auditory** person used **visual** language to communicate with the person who thinks with his eyes? *"Do you see what I mean?"*

Now that truly IS communication! When you start to do this you create tremendous rapport. It is a very powerful tool in terms of language. The more you practise it the sooner you will automatically know whether people see it, feel it or hear it.

People have been subconsciously aware of this for a long time – think about the next time you go to cross a railway line, you may see a sign that says STOP (kinaesthetic) LOOK (visual), LISTEN (auditory). Do you hear, see and feel what I'm saying?

There is a fourth communication preference called digital processing, or thinking. When digital communicators communicate they use language such as:

- *"Let me get my <u>head</u> round this"*
- *"Let me <u>sleep</u> on it"*
- *"I'm in two <u>minds</u>"*
- *"Let's <u>process</u> the facts"*

Digital communicators like to absorb information and process it before coming to a decision. They are people who sit back and think, managing to come up with the right comment at just the right time. Allowing them the pause to think and process builds rapport.

It is my belief the future will see a shift away from man-made technology into human technology, where we will be able to communicate by the power of thought. We will be able to remotely access what is happening thousands of miles away and we will start to use more than 10% of the human computer. These skills are used by indigenous populations and have been for thousands of years. Many of us have lost the ability to communicate in this way and we could learn a lot by going back to human basics.

Teaching Others

With this in mind, if you are going to teach a group of people how to do something you need to cover all four preferences – auditory, kinaesthetic, visual and digital:

1. Show them, and say nothing – **VISUAL**.
2. Then show them and then talk it through – **VISUAL** and **AUDITORY**.
3. Next, to get people to really learn you must ask *them* to talk it through – show **DIGITAL** understanding.
4. Finally, you get them to do it while talking it through. And roll together all four preferences – **VISUAL, AUDITORY, KINAESTHETIC** and **DIGITAL**.

That four point way of learning is a very powerful tool – it works whatever their communication preference, as I've discovered teaching thousands of students outdoor skills from climbing to sailing and extreme kayaking: If you take away just one of these preferences, be it visual, auditory or kinaesthetic, you dramatically reduce the power of your level of communication. You and I – all of us – need to communicate in all senses.

100% Communication

The way we take in information is also fascinating.

Amazing Fact Number Ten: Albert Mehrabian[12] (a UCLA professor) calculated that on average only 7% of the meaning attributed in communication is in the spoken WORD.

This suggests therefore that every time we write a letter, every time we send an e-mail, each time we send a text, we are missing out on a massive 93% of what we are trying to express! No wonder text messages are often misunderstood, need a little smiley face or down-turned mouth icon to impart true meaning. Words by themselves can be misleading. So too can punctuation! The title of the best seller 'Eats, Shoots, and Leaves' (Lynne Truss) implies hurried departure after a meal and an incident with a firearm whilst 'Eats Shoots and Leaves' refers to a panda thus taking on a different meaning entirely – and that's just with the use or omission of the odd comma!

So when it comes to words themselves, what are you to make of, for example, *'Thank you very much!'* – Was that meant as an honest thank you – or as a sarcastic reply meaning exactly the opposite?

ACTIVITY BOX

Both these passages contain exactly the same words but have very different meanings:

1. WOMAN WITHOUT HER MAN IS USELESS
2. WOMAN, WITHOUT HER, MAN IS USELESS

Amazing Fact Number Eleven: A further 38% of our communication is INTONATION; in the way we say the words and the speed, volume, rhythm and pitch of our speech.

Give it a go – try shouting 'RELAX!' at someone and see if they actually *do* relax! You can walk up to somebody with a big smile on your face and laughingly say "You're a real prat". The person will often smile back at you. But if you walk up with a grimace or a frown and say those same words with a downward inflection in your voice they may punch you!

This also demonstrates the remaining 55% of our communication – BODY LANGUAGE; our signals, what we say with our gestures, and the way we adorn ourselves. Therefore, when we listen to somebody on a radio we lose as much as half of the communication package because we can't see their body language. We can hear the words and feel the intonation in their voice but can only imagine their body language. It's the same when we communicate with people on the phone: we lose half the potential communication. When we are communicating with people we need to take in the whole package. For clarity we need 100% of that communication.

We need to examine how words, intonation and body language affect each other. People say that actions speak louder than words and that a picture paints a thousand words. If the words and the intonation don't match the body language there is no congruence. Have you ever heard somebody say *"I am really enjoying being here"* while actually shaking their head and subconsciously saying that they are not?

ACTIVITY BOX

Do this on someone:

While asking the following question hold one hand out moving it from side to side and wiggling your fingers as though reading Braille.

'What do deaf people read'

Often the answer will be 'Braille'. But the person is deaf, not blind! Which proves what? That <u>gestures</u> have more of an impact than the <u>words</u>. So remember when we communicate, body language is very important.

Common Body Language

If half our communication is with body language we need to be very aware of what that body language means. Within body language there are three elements – gestures, signals and adornments. The **signals/gestures** are the actions and body movements we perform. If you were to shout at a child and the child did not want to listen they would quickly put their hands over their ears. If you were to show a child or adult a dead rat and they did not want to see it, they would put their hands over their eyes. And if a child swore and knew they shouldn't have, they would quickly put their hand over their mouth. As adults, we use the same gestures but with more subtlety. If we don't want to say something, we will subconsciously put our hand up to our mouth or just below. If we don't want to hear something, we will subconsciously put our hand up to our ears, or scratch near our ear. If we don't want to see something we will put our hand up to our eyes by, for example, rubbing or scratching around them.

We use many gestures all the time, often subconsciously. We are not aware of our own gestures until we really, *really* start looking and taking notice of the movements and gestures of those around us.

Adornments refer to what people put on themselves that they didn't start off with in life – earrings, tattoos, a beard, moustache, even glasses. This also applies to the clothes that people choose to wear. Have you ever walked into a petrol station in a suit and been automatically asked by the cashier if you would like a VAT receipt, yet when you've walked into the same petrol station in a pair of jeans that question has been omitted? Give it a go. What we choose to 'put on' says a lot about who we feel we are, who we think we are and our perception of ourselves as well as the person we want other people to <u>think</u> we are. When you look at a person you see three people:

- The person they are
- The person you think they are
- The person they would like you to think they are

These perceptions are created through adornments, signals, gestures, verbal language and intonation.

The Importance of Space

Space is an important element in body language.

Amazing Fact Number Twelve: We each have an envelope of personal space that surrounds us. It's about 18 inches (45 cm) and it goes all around our body.

If anyone apart from a very close friend or partner comes into that space then they can very, very quickly erode our confidence and make us feel uncomfortable. This can be seen when we are having a meal – once seated we will play with our knives, forks, and napkin. Subconsciously, we arrange them to mark out our territory – watch others and you will see them doing it too. We may bring in our own wine glass or push it away – we are saying "This is my space. This is where I am sitting. This is who I am". As soon as we have done that we feel comfortable.

We can use this to our advantage: you can have a bit of fun with it too. By invading the 'territory' of someone sitting next to you or across from you it is possible to see whether you are building up a rapport and being accepted by them. When they are not looking, push your wine glass or another object which is yours, into *their* space. Subconsciously they will look down and say *"This isn't mine, this isn't mine"*. If they accept you they will keep it there, but if they don't, they will push it right back into your space.

Personal space is very important. In urban areas we tend to find it easier to be closer to people – just picture the underground at rush hour. In rural areas we want more space and need to be apart. When picnicking on the beach we will walk for ages looking for a larger patch of sand away from other people.

People can be habitual about space, sitting or standing in the same place in a particular area. This is because space represents emotional states both positive or negative. If you have ever seen somebody bang their hand down on a desk and say *"I am having a really, really bad time"*, the bad time is right where they have just banged their hand down. The last thing you want to do is go and put something of personal value, such as your work or company brochure, in that bad space because that space has become associated with negative feelings. In reference to the space that we stand in if you are giving a talk after another speaker, watch how the audience react to them. If they give a brilliant presentation and receive a great response, go and stand where they were standing. If they were not greatly received by the audience the last thing you want to do is stand in the same spot they did. The space they have just left is associated with negative performance.

First Impressions

Amazing Fact Number Thirteen: Body language experts such as Alan and Barbara Pease[13] suggest that 90% of your impression of a person will be made in the first four minutes. That's the first 240 seconds!

This applies not only when we first meet people but also when we see people that we know well: The first four minutes are absolutely key in any situation, for example meeting a friend, collecting children from school, or even just returning home from work to a loved one. A common gesture performed in the first four minutes is to shake hands and make eye contact. Therefore, we need to be really aware of how we perform these familiar gestures.

- **Handshake** This should be firm and confident but not aggressive.
  If your hand is on top of theirs it is saying you are more dominant than they are.
  If your hand is underneath theirs you are letting them dominate you.
  Ideally, you want to be on a level and have both hands side by side.

- **Space**   To stand too close is very domineering and can erode the other person's confidence.
  To stand too far away with your arm outstretched can lead to a lack of rapport and a feeling of distance.
- **Eye contact** Give approximately 5 seconds of eye contact. This will make the other person feel really good. Especially if you smile.
  If you find it difficult to look constantly into someone's eyes when they are speaking to you, move your eyes in a diamond shape over their face. First look at their forehead, then their left eye, their chin and finally their right eye.

When communicating with others we need to constantly read the signals they are giving out. You will notice that when people really like you, or like what you are saying, they will start pointing subconsciously towards you. This could be with any part of their body – for example they may cross their legs towards you, or point their feet in your direction. Their arms or their hands may point towards you, or their eye contact could be predominantly with you.

The Eyes

The eyes hold a lot of information about a person. They are the gateway to the mind and soul. Our eyes can show how confident we feel and if we are excited. If we turn away from someone with our eyes we are effectively saying "I am lacking in confidence." By giving lots of eye contact we are showing confidence and interest.

When you look somebody in the eye you can see how *they* are thinking. The visual hemisphere is at the top of the brain. The following points demonstrate how you can interpret a right handed person's eye movements:

- When people look up, they are tapping into their visual cortex.
- If people look up to their left, they are remembering an image.
- If they look up to their right, they are constructing an image.
- If people look in line with their left ear, their auditory cortex, they are remembering a sound.
- If they look in line with their right ear, they are constructing a sound.
- When people look down to their right they are getting in touch with their feelings. Have you ever heard anyone say *"I feel downright upset"*, *"I feel downright happy"*?

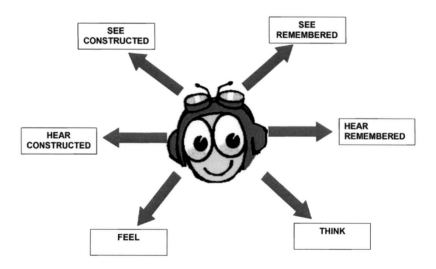

When people look down to their left they are talking to themselves – actually having a conversation.

So when we look at others we can very quickly look into their eyes and see where they are communicating. Obviously we are all individual – for a left handed person you can generally reverse the rules above, but there are always exceptions. You can check this by asking set questions at the beginning of a conversation and watching how the eyes move. This pioneering work was first created by Richard Bandler and John Grindler[14].

Eyes can also communicate our feelings. If someone is attracted to you or excited by what they see, their pupils will become dilated and will appear larger. That is why poker players often wear dark glasses: so as not to give away their hand of cards. And why you seldom see pandas playing poker!

In short, we can learn a great deal about how someone is feeling from their eyes – they are a very important form of communication, for they carry unspoken truths.

ACTIVITY BOX

Ask someone else these questions. Note where their eyes look. The eye movement may be very rapid.

1. What does a barking dog sound like? – Ear level to their left.
2. How do you feel when you see someone cry? – Down and to their left.
3. What is your age plus your best friend's age take away two? – up and to their right.
4. Picture the last time you were on a beach. – Up and to their left.
5. If your house had a fire alarm what would it sound like? – Ear level to their right unless their house does have a fire alarm and they are remembering instead of creating.

Listening

Listening is another really powerful communication tool. We have got two ears and only one mouth, suggesting we should perhaps use our ears twice as much as we use our mouth! When we really decide to listen, it engages people. In my seminars I ask people a sequence of questions to test their listening skills. As they pause ready for the last question I tell them there is no question but ask them to remember – at that moment – exactly what it feels like to be in that state: the state where they are absolutely 100% focused on listening. What many of us do is listen for the gaps in the conversation so that we can fill them with what <u>we</u> want to say. We say "Yes but...", and what we really mean is "*I have half listened to what you said but it is nothing like as interesting as what I have to say so now it is my turn to speak*". Consequently we haven't really listened to what the other person has said at all.

We can only take in so much information. Remember **Amazing Fact Number One**, back there in Chapter One? – The conscious mind can only take in 7 bits of information plus or minus 2, into the short term memory, at any one time. How many times have you met someone new and within the first four minutes find you have forgotten their name? (Four minutes? sometimes four *seconds*!). The reason for this is that you are communicating on a subconscious level. You are talking with people and listening to them, smelling how they smell, taking in how they look. Make sure that person's name is one of those 7 bits of information. To remember a person's name is very important. If you are a Visual, write it down or create an image of that person's name. If you are an Auditory or Verbal create a phonic clue to aid your memory. When you meet that person again and you remember their name, it makes them feel important. If we really listen to what is being said to us and we rapidly repeat it in our heads, it will help us to remember.

Close your Autobiography

Listening to others opens up channels of communication. It produces feelings of empathy, which lead to goodwill between people. It is very important to listen to others rather than just prescribe out of your own autobiography (Stephen Covey[3]). It is all too easy to prescribe out of our experiences, drone on about what <u>we</u> have done and what <u>we</u> think other people should do. Put away that waggling finger! It is because everyone is unique, that we need to really *listen* to others, and hear their story. So next time, before you trundle out the autobiography and drone on with all those sentences that begin with "When I" (when I did this, when I did that) ask yourself – 'What do I need to do for this person? How can I help them? What do they need? What would it feel like if I did this?'

We have a habit of playing a game known as 'black catting' (Paul 'Bullet' Turner[15]) – *"Oh yes I have done that too"* and *"When I did that….".* It creates the impression that you are always trying to be one up on the other person, trying to make yourself feel good and not listening to what they are actually saying. Instead, turn the tables. Listen. Really listening to people gives a great sense of rapport and understanding. Imagine how it would make you feel if someone really listened to you, wanted to completely understand what you were saying before making themselves understood. Do this next time you're in serious conversation. Notice the change. Notice that it creates an amazing feeling of empathy, of closeness. It makes people want to communicate with you even more because – hey – talking to you is suddenly a really pleasurable experience! Of course, conversation is a dialogue – you do need to get your point across too: you don't want to stare at them, listening so intently that you look as though you're a startled rabbit! But active, sensitive listening enables you to make a more sensitive contribution to the conversation.

Good active listening also involves repeating back to that person what they have just said. Use their language. In the same way that we talked about visual, auditory and kinaesthetic you can use their language without paraphrasing what they say. If someone says *"I have had a great day"* and you reply *"I'm so glad you've had a good day"* you are not showing complete understanding. You need to use their word 'great' instead! If you can do this, if you can really listen and become interested in people, they will automatically become more interested in you. You only get back what you give out.

Remember: two ears, one mouth. We must be built that way for a reason, don't you think? I'm listening now, really carefully, for your reply.

Understanding

When communicating with someone on a VHF radio you say their name three times to get their attention followed by your name three times to ensure they know who it is. Saying things three times massively helps the information to be understood. Think about the news, they tell you what you are going to hear, they then tell you in detail and then summarise by telling you what you have been told.

Another aid to understanding is questioning what you have been told. We all naturally make assumptions about communications. And we all know what happens when we assume! (makes an ASS of U and ME).

ACTIVITY BOX

Please read the following and picture it in your head:

There was a mountaineer, on a 45 degree slope. They were climbing higher and higher, using ice axes and crampons. The wind was whipping up snow and ice around the mountain. The mountaineer reached a level and quickly put up their tent. The mountaineer then got into the tent and after taking their rucksack off, crawled into their sleeping bag and got out a hot drink.

1. Was the mountaineer male or female?
2. What colour was their clothing?
3. What colour was their tent?
4. What was the mountaineer drinking?

The mountaineer was female; she was wearing yellow and red; the tent was orange and grey and she was drinking tea.

See how we assume and prescribe from our own autobiography?

I would be surprised if you or the other person next to you got the same answers. There was just a series of words. There was no explanation and no description, so the words are entirely open to interpretation – and wrong assumption. It goes to show that when we communicate with people we need to be really clear; we need to ask questions to check understanding.

Do:
- Actively listen to others.
- Read people's body language for signals and react to it.
- Use the language of those you are communicating with to build rapport.
- Say things three times.

Remember:
We communicate through visual, auditory, kinaesthetic and digital (sight, sound, touch and thinking).

Body language is over <u>half</u> our communication.

Do not presume others can see, feel and hear the same concept as you, the same way as you.

Notes

Notes

CHAPTER FOUR

Queen Bee

(Personal Leadership)

'Cutting Edge!'

Think about a person that you can trust, rely on and would want to be with in a difficult situation. Rob is one such person and it's no surprise that with these qualities he has become a top plastic surgeon.

His personal leadership and integrity give him a passion to work in the highest areas of mental, physical and emotional challenge. Once you open up a human being to operate on them it demands the ultimate personal and team leadership to remain focused, calm and confident in your abilities and of those around you.

Rob sets out clear vision before every operation. He is a brilliant people person and puts people at ease. His personality is magnetic and fun. His operations are slick, calm and cutting edge! They are proactive, dynamic and above all fun – fun you say? Without fun Rob could not operate – the sense of fun takes the edge off a potentially frightening environment.

He is one of the most competent and unassuming people that I have ever met. Someone you would literally trust your life with! It is ultimate leadership when people go under the surgeon's knife.

His greatest leadership skill is that he really cares for people and this shows in his continued commitment to be involved in making people's lives better for them. What a gift to give to others.

Do you Run your Life or does Life Run You?

Quantum mechanics is about the field of possibility; we should make it our business to be focused on the possible. The future is a good place to get into, for it is where we spend the rest of our lives! Most people, however, focus on the past, upon what has gone and cannot be recalled rather than the infinite excitement of what lies ahead: Do what you have always done and you will get what you have always got. Do something new, however, push the boundaries, do something positive and experience the difference.

So – think now and think hard about changing the way you do things. Why? Because we all want to be better, we all want to feel good about our performance, and make the best of every single chance we get. Above all, start to be really aware that you CAN DO so many of the things that other people say you can't. A common element that I have noticed wherever I teach is a lack of self-belief. It's tragic. For without self-belief there can be no genuine self-confidence. But with self-belief there *is* confidence, sure as night follows day.

Have you ever had a negative experience and thought "I'm never doing *that* again, the same thing will happen again"? This can stifle your personal leadership – the way you lead and develop yourself. It can cause you to shy away from new adventures and the thrill of new rewards.

Confidence Vs. Arrogance

Have you ever been told not to be cocky or too confident, causing you to play down your abilities? In the world today when we are good at something we run the risk of being called an arrogant show off. But there is a difference, in my book, between arrogance and confidence. Arrogance is <u>thinking</u> you can do something and confidence is <u>knowing</u> you can. Many people today have lost their self-belief and confidence and this has had a knock on effect on our society. We need to change the way we see ourselves to increase our sense of well-being and inner self-worth.

Confidence is determined by:

- Our environment
- Our experiences
- The people that we *choose* to surround us
- The relationships that we *choose*
- The attitudes we *choose* to have

Look at these areas in your life: place of work, and home. The people who surround us, day in, day out. The relationships we choose to nourish, foster or ignore. Do you lead these elements or are you led by them? Do they knock you down, sap your confidence, and make every step a trudge? Look at your self-image. That's it – you. Right there. The man or woman in the mirror. Do you like what you see?

Through positive personal leadership you have the power to better manage the above elements causing them to affect your confidence and self-esteem in a good way. People will always treat you the way you treat yourself. If you sabotage yourself and tell yourself that you <u>can't</u> do things, subconsciously you tell others that you are unable. If you believe you are not as good as other people, then that is the signal and message you send out. Very quickly others will believe them too. Horses, they say, smell fear. Humans too, I believe, detect unerringly the aura of self-doubt, of self-disbelief in those around them. Anyone you know a self-doubter?

Talk to yourself positively. Tell yourself you can, you will, and you'll do it. The language you use to talk to yourself and to others must be reinforced by your body language.

In The Words of Aretha Franklin R-E-S-P-E-C-T

When the chips are down, when you're in the tightest of tight corners, YOU will be the best friend you'll ever have, the one person you'll know you can rely on to look after your best interests. So – make an investment now: look after yourself; get to know who you really are; develop. And to develop you need, first of all, to respect yourself. You need to really *like* yourself and want to constantly improve that inner and outer you. The greatest need of human beings is to be loved, valued and needed. We also have a need to constantly improve our environment, relationships and ourselves. There is a brilliant saying:

> *"The only part of the universe that you are 100% guaranteed of changing is yourself"*
>
> A. Huxley[16]

My motto is *"We need to look after number one in order to look after number two"*, or put another way, we need to be selfish to be selfless. If we can learn to put more into ourselves, then what we give to others is of far better quality. While out walking on the mountains if you are cold, wet and miserable you are in no position to look after anyone you are with.

Do you see yourself as a role model? Think about it. This is a very important concept to explore. If we can be role models, if we can really improve what we do and how we do it, then we give off all the right signals to others. How do we do that? First, we need to know where we are *right now*. Overleaf is a development wheel. Each spoke represents an important area in life. Have you ever ridden a bicycle with a broken spoke? Even if all the other spokes are there, with one gone the balance is upset and the wheel can still buckle. We can apply this same theory to life – we need to create a balance, we need all the spokes on our personal development wheel.

By filling in the wheel below, you can easily see the areas in your life that you feel are sorted, and the areas that need work. On each spoke give yourself a score out of ten. A fulfilled life would be represented by a full wheel. This exercise will highlight the areas of your life that need more time, care or attention. Focus on them now and improve your own life-balance by self-awareness. You can also get someone who knows you well to fill it in on your behalf to compare their perception with yours.

Development Wheel

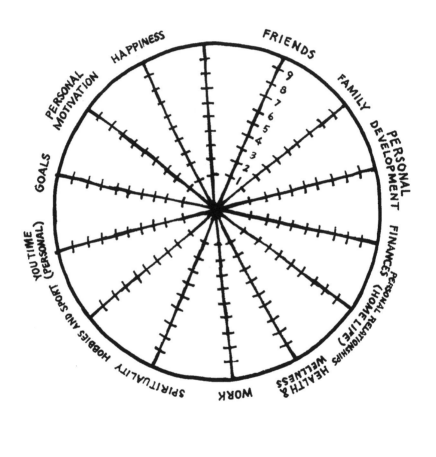

Understanding our values and beliefs is important to personal leadership. Those values and beliefs represent **who** we are and **why** we are. They look at our inner self in terms of: "What is our purpose? Why are we here? What do we believe in?" We need to realise which beliefs are stronger than others and what values we have for our lives. Those values might be integrity, they might be honesty, they might be to love, or they might be to give. But if the values and the beliefs contradict each other, that basic contradiction can lead to a lot of stress in life. One of your beliefs might be that you want to be a teacher but if you have a value that you really don't like young people you are going to have conflict (Just a bit!). And that would lead to stress. The values and beliefs need to be congruent. They need to be in line with one another, otherwise you experience cognitive dissonance – an incompatibility of your values and beliefs.

So – what is personal leadership? Personal leadership is how we decide to set direction in our lives – it's the vision that we have for our lives. Where we are going to go, how we are going to get there, why we want to get there, and what it will feel like, look like and sound like when we arrive.

And our movement towards that distant objective needs to be supported by asking yourself – and answering – the following key questions: "Self ", you say –

- How motivated am I?
- How do I communicate with myself?
- How happy am I?
- How disciplined am I?
- How skilled am I with my emotional intelligence?

Stop now and take time out to write down honest answers to these questions.

Welcome back!

Emotional Intelligence

We all have the ability to be intelligent but many only focus on the notion of IQ, such as mathematical aptitude, logical ability and verbal reasoning. Researchers are now saying that this makes up only 20% of our true intelligence – which is really good news for those of us who glazed over at the back of the class during algebra. 80% of our *true* intelligence is made up of *emotional* intelligence. Emotional intelligence is:

> *"...the learned ability to perceive, to understand and to express our feelings accurately."*
>
> Daniel Goleman[17]

It is how we control our emotions so that they work *for* us and not against us. However, the key to personal success is using our emotional quotient with our intellectual quotient together, in tandem.

IQ + EQ = SUCCESS

By using the two together we make up our total intelligence.

There are two areas to emotional intelligence: **The intra-personal and the inter-personal.**

The Intra-personal

Our inner intelligence – how we know, how we understand, how we motivate ourselves. It's about self-awareness, self motivation and emotional management.

The Inter-personal

The other side is how we interact with other people – the outer intelligence, our *inter*-personal skills. How we read and sense and understand; our abilities in terms of relationship management and emotional coaching. This plays a massive role in our personal leadership – how we lead ourselves in order to get the best out of others. Gardner and Goleman[18] describe these facets of our intelligence.

- **Self-awareness** is your ability to see yourself through your own eyes, to be aware of your goals, your beliefs, your values, your rules and your self-talk.
- **Emotional management** is the ability to identify the interaction between your thoughts, feelings and actions. So, what you think, how you feel, what you do. Aristotle wrote that anyone can become angry, that's easy. But to be angry with the right person, to the right degree, at the right time, for the right purpose and in the right way – that is not easy.
- **Self motivation** is the ability to pursue your goals with commitment, passion and perseverance – which is all fine and dandy if you're there already. But if you're not – then how do you get really motivated? We will look at that later on when we focus on what you want to do and how you are going to do it.
- **Relationship management** is the ability to effectively manage your relationships with others and to build effective networks: Team building and relationship building.
- **Emotional coaching** is the ability to help others develop their emotional capabilities, to resolve differences, to solve problems, to communicate effectively and to get other people motivated, to lead people into that way of thinking, that way of feeling and that way of doing.

With those very powerful thoughts in mind you can start to focus. If you start to focus on yourself, you are then equipped to focus on others.

Really look at the sort of person you want to become. I believe that often involves modelling other people's actions. Look at how other people are and ask yourself:

- What is it that I really like about that person?
- What is it that I really want to emulate so I can become similar to them?
- What do they do? How do they do it? If I can imitate it, will it have the same impact?

Start to look around and see what it is that people do that works for them. Then start to model that behaviour for yourself remembering, that because no two people are ever exactly alike, there will never be a perfect fit or comparison. The more you can do this, the more other people will want to model their behaviour on you. And, Hey Presto! Before you know it, you too will be a role model. Good news, eh?

Making Mistakes

Making mistakes is a positive step towards learning. Too many people are too frightened to move out of their comfort zones and make mistakes. Why? Because they fear *faillllllllllure*! We talked about people having a fear of failure and also a fear of success, because to be too successful is not within their map or model of the world. If we can make mistakes, we can really learn from them. It is not, however, a particularly good thing to repeat the same mistake over and over again! Learning from our actions, doing things differently as a result of our mistakes – now that IS a very powerful and positive thing. Some people say that to treble your successes you must treble your failures, which again is about getting out of your comfort zones and accepting that mistakes are all part of the process. So unzip that comfort zone, take a deep breath and…..get out there!

Will Power

To lead ourselves, we have to focus on our will power. We can measure this for everything we do. Next time you're thinking about priorities, put a mark out of ten against how much you want to achieve a particular task. How much do you want to reach that self-chosen goal?

If your will to achieve is less than 5 out of 10 – forget it: you're wasting your time. That goal will never be achieved. So, before you set yourself any task, rise to meet any challenge, ask yourself this: "What is my will to achieve?"

```
0 ——————————— 5 ——————————— 10
Nil will          Some will          All your will
```

How disciplined are you? What time do you put in to being disciplined? Or do you allow yourself to go off the boil? Do you allow yourself to just relax, then tell yourself "Well, I don't really have to worry about that?" Do you lose focus?

To be disciplined, to absolutely agree that you are going to behave in a certain way is easy to say, but hard to do. The first thing we need to do is *think* about those 21 days it takes to get into a habit, a pattern of different activity. You need to know that if you do something over and over again it becomes easier; the more you do something, the easier it becomes. The brain is like a muscle and so to develop it we need to do things over and over again; until we do it in a way that becomes almost unconsciously competent – a way that simply happens naturally.

Skill Development

As we learn a process we go through various stages of development. (Bateson 1973[19])

- When we first learn to do things, we don't know what we are doing. We are **UNCONSCIOUSLY INCOMPETENT**. We don't know if we are going to be good at it or not.
- After we have had a bit of practice, we suddenly become **CONSCIOUSLY INCOMPETENT** as we realise we are not as good as we thought we were. For example, learning to drive. To start with you put your foot on the brake and almost

go through the windscreen! Suddenly, you realise you are not a natural, not as good as you thought you were going to be.

- Then, as you practice more and more, you pass your test and you move into a situation where you become **CONSCIOUSLY COMPETENT**. You are aware of what you do, you think about it, you bring it to your conscious attention. You are now in the **awareness zone**.
- Finally when many of us drive, we are in that zone where we are **UNCONSCIOUSLY COMPETENT**. On automatic pilot. We often get to places and think: How did I get here? How did I arrive here? We know what we are doing to such an extent that we do things without having to think about them – sometimes without realising that we're even doing them at all!

That is a good way to work, but it's also a good idea to step back into the **consciously competent** stage where you are really aware how you are. This skill is about being disciplined, about checking and reviewing your behaviour. The hard thing is starting. Once you do it that first time then, with each repetition, it becomes easier. Soon, the right action has become hard-wired into the brain and it happens automatically.

The challenge for many of us is that the wrong habits get hard-wired. We get into lazy habits and set up a pattern of saying to ourselves "*I'll do it sometime*" with that "sometime" often meaning never. We get into the habit of saying "*I don't really want to get out of bed early this morning*". We put ourselves in situations which in the end become hard-wired as bad habits and unproductive patterns of behaviour.

Look at different ways of doing things. We all have a perspective from our own point of view. But if you can look at a situation through another person's eyes, take it from a second perspective, then it becomes very different. By doing this we become disassociated with how *we* feel and open our minds to different points of view. If you can take that perspective from a <u>third</u> set of eyes, then it becomes even more disassociated and you can have a totally altered 'take' on what is happening. Mahatma Gandhi[20] would see things from three different perspectives; from a Hindu viewpoint, from a Muslim viewpoint and from a Christian viewpoint. When you are able to see things from many different viewpoints, feel things in many different ways and hear things from differing angles, <u>then</u> you can allow yourself to change.

What Makes You Happy?

All of us are crying out for one single simple thing. Know what it is? To be happy. Jean Vanier[21] wrote:

> *"What do we really want? To be happy, to know happiness, is the great desire of every man and woman. We may differ perhaps in the means by which we obtain happiness, but we all want to be happy. This is our great aspiration."*

What makes us happy? Well, for many people it is putting time into the things that are most important to us, be that family, health, work, or relationships. We need to really focus on what makes us happy. In terms of looking at our own personal leadership we should focus our attentions and energies on the things that make us feel good. Focus on what we really want to do, rather than on what we don't want to do. Tragically, many of us get this wrong.

Action in Crisis

Another important part of personal leadership is dealing with situations when suddenly things start to go wrong. Do you react or respond to a crisis? Can we, when everything around us seems to be going pear-shaped, keep a cool head? Can we keep calm, can we keep relaxed, can we keep our mind and physiology in control so that we don't run around doing that celebrated impression of a headless chicken? To put time into that skill – learning to be cool under pressure – is pretty hard because we don't generally get into those situations. But it is a really important area to think about, to imagine, and to play over in our mind's eye. How would we react in an emergency situation? Plan for it, anticipate it, think through your actions, visualise what you would do in particular situations, and there's a much better chance that, under pressure, you'll maintain that cool.

Victor Frankl[22] was a prisoner in a German prisoner of war camp who was experimented on time and time again. He realised that they could harm his whole body, but the one thing they couldn't take away was his mind, his ability to keep calm and positive in the face of adversity. And it's that which I think is so important: that inner kernel of self-discipline and self-belief.

Every single one of us gets stressed and yet – and here's **Amazing Fact Number Fourteen** – every fifteen minutes the body naturally goes into shut-down mode. It's a time when you find yourself daydreaming or just wanting to relax. Yet we often override that daydream.

As a result, we rarely give ourselves time to relax and unwind, so instead we suffer from stress until it becomes an illness. In order for us to deal with this, we need to allow time for relaxation. Relaxation means different things to different people. It may be getting out and changing your environment, getting outdoors or being indoors; it may be reading, praying or just taking the cat for a walk. Whatever does it for you, you need to find out. And then do it.

Work Life Balance

We also need to put time into looking after ourselves. Do you eat properly? Do you eat enough of the right things, at the right time? Do you feel good within yourself? Do you eat enough fruit, do you eat enough vegetables, do you get enough of the right proteins, fats and carbohydrates, the right amount of minerals? What about caffeine? Do you drink enough water? Does your body crave water? Are you living your life permanently dehydrated? If our bodies are getting enough of the right nutrients it allows us to be far more effective. Sleep is also of major importance. Do you sleep enough? Do you take enough time out, not for others, but for yourself? It is vitally important to take time out to do the things that make you feel good – spending time with friends and family, exercising, holidays and hobbies.

Do:
- Build your confidence.
- Create a work/life balance.
- Become a role model.
- Fill out a life wheel on a monthly basis.
- Maintain personal discipline.

Remember:
Focus on what you want.

Work on your emotional intelligence.

Notes

Notes

CHAPTER FIVE

Make Honey

(Relationships)

'Lasting Impression'

Opportunities always come along – it's often our choice to make them and take them or leave them and grieve them.
In 1989 a friend sent me a newspaper cutting:

Position vacant – Senior instructor in an outdoor centre Devon with a mixture of field studies.

I had just finished teaching geography and had a background in the outdoors. So I applied, took the train to Devon and was picked up by Chris. During the interview Chris and Iain (the owner of the centre) said they had actually given the job to someone else. I managed however to talk Iain into letting me have the senior post and suggested the other applicant could run the field studies. After I had bombarded Iain with what we could do to develop the centre he stopped and said *"Look here Jack you can't just come down here and tell me to do this and that! I have been here for 15 years."* Anyway he liked my enthusiasm and gave me the job.

Iain is a massively talented outdoors man, skier, sailor and kayaker. He gave me a huge opportunity to work once more in the outdoors – he trusted me and gave me wonderful experiences. We had a great friendship. Sadly in 2005 Iain was diagnosed with cancer and has been given six months to a year to live. This reminds me to live life to the full, 'Carpe Diem'!

We all have relationships with people, work with them, love them, and value them. Iain will never know what he gave me that day he took me on. Some years later he came on a two day programme I ran called 'Will Power'. I was touched that he attended – a man full of fun, skill and great thinking. Thanks for the good times, Iain, I owe you so much and hope I can give back to others what you gave me.

Relationships. They're the glue that holds life together. Whether they're working, failing, building or falling apart, our relationships with others form a major part of our lives. But maintaining these relationships with loved ones, friends or work colleagues, requires nurturing and effort.

Stages of Development

We all start off in life as DEPENDENT – we need to be looked after. We need to be fed and cared for. Without that care and support we cannot survive. The years tick on by, we stop chucking the baked beans at the kitchen wall, get a grip on potty training and before you can say 'spots' – we're teenagers. When we reach our teenage years we find ourselves striving to become INDEPENDENT. We don't really need other people, we can do most things on our own and we want to break free from the help and, as we see it, stifling constraint, of others. Finally we make our way into the later stages of our lives, the stage of needing other people, of being INTERDEPENDENT and needing to be part of a team, part of a group. Steven Covey[3] describes this in more detail in his books.

It's a little bit like a river; the river starts off in its youth, it doesn't quite know where it's going as it attempts to find the quickest way down, regardless of what's in the way. It runs fast, barges things aside, knocks things down in its haste. Then as the river proceeds, in the middle stages, it carves out its path and looks at where it's going and how it's going to get there. Then finally, in the last stages of maturity, the river starts to become slower and deeper. It is far more responsible. It lays down its deposits to support other parts of life. Now it's giving back to the land: the taking days are over. Which, if you like, is rather how we should try to live our lives. We should think about how we take and how we give back to life. When we are younger we need to take, then we carry on and are able to choose our own course, our own direction. But, perhaps we should think more about what we put back.

In Britain today, roughly one marriage in three breaks down – and behind that bald statistic lies tears and pain, anger, deceit and broken dreams. So what can <u>we</u> do differently to change that, give those dreams a better chance? When looking at the past chapters we see we have to look after number one in order to look after number two. In fact, as you've seen, we have to be selfish to be selfless. If we can look after, invest and work on ourselves and learn to love ourselves, then we can give more to others. As it says in The Bible: "Love thy neighbour as thyself."

Relationship Development

Bruce Tuckman's 1965[23] *'Forming, Storming, Norming and Performing'* Team Development Model can be used to look at relationship development and management.

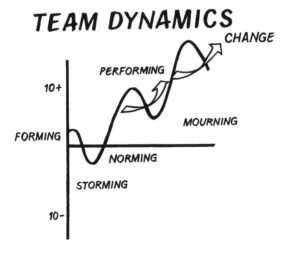

FORMING – When people come together in any kind of a team, they FORM. They get to know one another and their behaviours are often accommodating. They are polite as they analyse each other.

STORMING – As the team get to know one another they tend to learn about the idiosyncrasies and behaviours that make them what they are. They test each other to learn the boundaries of how far they can push them. These can cause upset, annoyance and arguments, the team is starting to STORM.

NORMING – As the team spend time together they begin to accept or understand the behaviour of each other. Group norms are created, such as a common language and rituals. These then become set, and roles within the group are allocated and defined either formally or informally.

PERFORMING – With a mutual understanding of people's roles the team start to feel grounded with a sense of togetherness. Finally, the team PERFORM and work well together.

Performing teams that peak can find themselves in a precarious environment. Once you get to the top of your game there is a tendency to relax, this relaxation can be dangerous as the only way is down. In this environment motivation can fade alongside performance. Many mountaineers die on the top of mountains having reached their goal of summiting. They relax, lose focus, and make deadly mistakes. Think about how much effort you put into a new relationship compared to two years down the line…feel familiar? It is at this peak that people can get complacent and go into a MOURNING stage. To stop this loss in performance the solution is to continually strive for new goals and constant improvement. This relates to our everyday lives be they personal, or working relationships.

Team Roles

Is that 'storming' phase inevitable? Must we go through that to reach performance? For many of us the key lies in understanding: understanding each other, understanding which buttons to press (although I have never found that little sign that says please press here!) and saying, *"What can I do to get the best out of that person?"* Doctor Meredith Belbin[24] realised that we all have different roles in teams and groups. As with communication, individuals have preferences towards certain roles. Some people like to lead a team, others prefer to concentrate on the detail ensuring that the t's are crossed and the i's are dotted. A bit like a car engine, we may not know all of the parts but if you remove just one component, a carburettor for example, the engine will not run. In the same way high performance teams, Belbin suggests, need to have a blend of eight roles to make the team work. In many relationships be they teams, groups or personal, people choose or select others in their own likeness. We are drawn towards those that are similar to us. Does this ring true for you? I worked with a large team of technically brilliant nurses with low team performance only to discover that they all had very similar skill sets. Having recognised the roles that were missing they were able to build on their skills and bring in new team members to increase performance. We all have the ability to be the Jack of all trades but we cannot be a master of all. We excel by realising what we are good at and working on the things that we could be better at.

Celebrate Different Talents

One of the most important things that I can put in this book is the ability to understand what makes others tick. Basic psychology enables us to be aware of people's make-up, their values, their beliefs, their preferences and their paradigms. Many people have not looked or attempted to really understand why others do what they do. Even after twenty years of working together people can arrive at an 'Aha' moment on courses…*"Now I get it"*…. *"Now I see why he does that"* ….*"That explains it!"* Once we have that understanding we are able to be a lot more tolerant of others, and patient towards them.

Belbin is one of many psychologists who gives us an insight into how people behave and work with others. By understanding these different roles we can use people's skills to the advantage of the relationship and have greater patience when they don't work in exactly the same way we do.

The secret to successful relationships and teams is:

- To like who you work with and love those who are close to you.
- Have a passion and a vision for what you do, what you need to achieve and where you are going.
- Have a variety of different talents, and roles.
- Different skills, knowledge and attitudes.
- The ability to understand each other and speak the same language.
- Empathy.
- Mutual trust and support.
- A desire for positive outcomes.

This development process is based on really listening to, understanding and feeling what people are saying. By taking the time to listen and understand we will find it easier to be understood by others also. We need to listen to other perspectives. It's not about listening to people and trying to solve their problems, or telling people very quickly what they need to do. If we want to *really* listen to people then we have to ask the right questions. Questions like *"How do you know that?" "What does that make you feel like?"* Listen to people in terms of what <u>they</u> see happening, what <u>they</u> hear themselves doing and then look at it from their perspective rather than from your own.

You might have noticed that I use the word 'need' regularly. That is because needs are necessities and wants are wishes.

Amazing Fact Number Fifteen: Statistics suggest that we give five bits of negative information to every one bit of positive (and we all know that 99% of statistics are all made up on the spot!).

People around us need to be loved, valued, needed and wanted. We do too! Tell people: *'I respect what you do'*, *'I like what you do'*, *'I appreciate what you have done'*. It has an *incredible* effect upon them – notice it in their body language and in the manner in which they turn towards you. We need to focus upon praising people rather than putting them down. Why is it, I wonder, that sometimes putting people down, concentrating upon the negative, seems to have become a thriving cottage industry? Make a start and make a difference: right now, concentrate on the positive in the next person you talk to.

Synergy

The desire to have your own way often leads to conflict. Think of two people in a room – one of them wants to put the stereo on while the other person wants silence: One says keep it off, the other – turn it on. If the stereo is turned on you have a win-lose situation. You achieve the same result if it is turned off. If those two people really look at the situation, what they need to do is ask the questions: "Why do you want the stereo on?" And "Why do you want it off?" The answers may be: *"Well, I want the radio on to listen to the weather report and see if it is windy enough to go kite surfing"*, and *"I want the stereo off because I have a migraine and it will make it worse"*. So you have conflict: on – off, off – on. We want to avoid a situation where both lose.

If you have a battle, both parties end up feeling uncomfortable and guilty. It is not just about compromise, it is about synergy – creating a situation in which the end result has greater value than the two separate situations added together. Synergy would say: let's turn on the radio and give the person who wants to listen headphones so the migraine-sufferer cannot hear it. Bingo! Now you have arrived somewhere much better. You have a win-win situation. How many times have you noticed circumstances where people never really get the best deal? We need to create better outcomes for ourselves – and for others. We must ensure people realise how much we value them by the positive language we use towards them.

Invest in What you Have

As with teams in any relationship we tend to get to the top where we peak and perform and then subsequently get comfortable. Remember the mountaineers and their deadly mistakes. When relationships get too comfortable we can get complacent. People no longer give so much thought to the things they do and this is when we can find ourselves in a place of risk where we can start to lose people – and relationships – because it takes effort to be understanding. We need to constantly maintain that point where we are always striving to reach the top but are not quite there. To keep the momentum going requires great effort so that we are constantly re-peaking and improving what we do.

Too many times people say that the grass is greener elsewhere and they look from one valley to the other. They will say *"It looks better over there"*. This can stop us putting real time into the people we are with. If we invest in the people around us, then we can make a real difference. Give someone five bits of positive feedback every day for a week and notice their change in attitude towards you. Perhaps that is one of the strongest messages – that we need to put time into the people that we have got and really invest in them, rather than take the easy option of letting them go and looking for someone else on a greener patch of grass. I believe that this is becoming a massive epidemic in our 'discard' society today. But people aren't crisp packets or tin cans to be tossed aside the moment they're used up or have ceased performing. They're creatures of infinite worth with huge potential just waiting to be discovered. We need to focus on emotional intelligence, how we deal with relationships, how we deal with the ability to coach other people and understand how they are feeling. Take the time to find out what it is that makes them feel good or bad.

It is all too easy in our society to know – and exploit – the Achilles heel, the weaknesses people have. Almost by default, we put people under pressure, then wonder and shake our heads if they start to buckle. Perhaps it's time we tried something different. Perhaps instead we should support them, help them face any issues and deal with those issues of challenge head-on.

Your personal integrity is crucial – do you trust yourself and can you be trusted; how honest are you, and can you be completely open with the people that matter in your life. This is key when breaking down some of those barriers that have perhaps held us back in relationships. We need to open up and allow our better selves to work with people. We should show them our strengths, even let them into some of our weak areas, some of those areas where we know we can improve. By being open in this way we create a tremendous amount of rapport and an atmosphere of openness and mutual support.

So many people lack confidence and self-belief. They think they lack all sorts of things other people have, yet we all have so many gifts, so many qualities. The fact that we are just breathing and living on this planet is an amazing feat – whatever state our bodies are in. We're lucky to be here. So enjoy the experience. Go with it and let life happen in a positive way. Play your music.

Create Rapport

Be aware of how people send out signals and gestures. Be aware of what people do and say. Think about how you create rapport with people; listen to how they communicate – be that by visual, auditory, kinaesthetic or digital means. Repeat their language back to them. Get people to say 'yes' and get people to come on board. Use language such as 'yes tags' that allow people to say yes. For example if I said *"Can you drive?"* and you can, then you would probably say "Yes." And it would feel easy doing that, wouldn't it? It's a good thing to say yes, isn't it? It makes you feel good, doesn't it? So use the sort of language that makes people say yes rather than no. If you said to somebody, *"I don't suppose you want a cup of tea?"* The answer would be predisposed to be no, but if you said, *"You probably want a cup of tea, don't you?"* then, guess what? The answer would probably be yes.

The pre-disposition of your question allows people to say yes. So create rapport with people in terms of:

- How you say things
- The way you speak
- The language you use
- By your smile
- By actually *listening* to people; by finding out what makes them tick, what it is that is really important to them.

People love talking about themselves. Find out what they do and ask them about themselves. And do so <u>before</u> you tell them about yourself.

When we are in teams, people mirror our behaviour. If people feel open towards us they will move closer and their bodies will be more open. Their eyes will be dilated if they enjoy what we are talking about. They will smile more, laugh more. If people enjoy rapport with us they will do things that make us feel good, so we must make people feel good. Let's be absolutely aware that everything we throw out in terms of relationships will be like the boomerang. What we throw out we get back. Treat people as you want yourself to be treated. Really think about the law of ten fold: what you put out you get back ten times over. If you can *really* learn to give to other people, to become massively interested in other people, to focus on looking after other people, then it starts to come back to you. And it does so in a massive way.

Do:
- Look at what you take and what you give back.
- Tell people what you like about them.
- Create win – win situations.
- Put time into the people around you instead of looking elsewhere for new relationships.
- Be aware of the storming stage in relationships and teams so that you can work through it.

Remember:
Relationships need to be nurtured and worked on.

Avoid complacency.

Notes

Notes

CHAPTER SIX

Get the Pollen

(Goals)

How young are you!?

Tell Jim you are too old to do things, and watch him laugh at you – with good reason. At 54 years young he spent nine eventful months at sea and travelled from South America to Queensland to become the first person to ever row single handed across the Pacific Ocean!

In the tradition of great and often eccentric travellers he overcame endless obstacles in reaching his goal. From the blank refusal of Chilean officials to let him start because they believed he had no chance of success, to forgetting a can opener! His journey was full of hazards that would have stopped many hardy adventures – fending off sharks with make-shift harpoons, his communication equipment failed, he was 10 metres from being crushed by an oil tanker and hurricane Paula nearly took his life.

Jim is a legend – he set himself the goal he knew he could achieve and did. I love his charismatic big personality that says "I can". He appears on our annual Rotary Youth Leadership Award programme as a guest speaker. The delegates love his down to earth and engaging manner – putting the powerful message in their minds that age only holds us back if we let it.

To see how he fulfilled his dream goal read **Shekhdar, Jim**. *Bold Man of the Sea: My Epic Journey* (2001) Hodder & Stoughton.

The power to achieve our goals lies in the power of our mind.

Goals. But not as in football.

Have you ever got lost while driving or out walking? This loss of direction often leads to a lack of confidence! Once we have checked our map and we are back on track we feel more in control. Right now, it's a good time to get our life map out.

How many times have you heard yourself or others say "I should", "ought to", "might", "could" or "try to" with their goals?

Let me share with you the 'will', 'must', 'when', 'can' and 'how to'.

For some years I had the goal to write this book. I knew what to do; I knew how to do it but was challenged by the DO. I asked myself what was stopping me and the simple answer was me. So I focused on two areas, pain and gain; how much pain would my inaction cause me and how much gain would my action bring. Very quickly I realised that it had to be achieved, more to move away from the pain than to achieve the gain. I also realised that I had to stop telling people that I was going to write a book, as people only give you so much time to achieve something before they start to doubt you.

A goal is a future action. The future is a good place to get interested in, as it's where we will spend the rest of our lives! Why live in the past?

Of course it's made us who we are but it's gone: the future's about to happen.

Your mind is like a heat-seeking missile: what you aim and focus at is where you go.

People often say I don't want to put on weight, be unhappy or get ill.

What do they get? Overweight, unhappy and ill. If we change our focus to what we want, we get to be fit, happy and well!

With this focus in mind, what are your short term, medium and long term goals?

Amazing Fact Number Sixteen: A study at Harvard University[25], in the USA, found that within a year group only 3% of students formally set goals and 97% chose not to. Researchers monitored all the students for ten years. They found that the 3% with real goals were tangibly richer financially, physically, mentally, emotionally and spiritually than the 97% who went through life without any!

To formally set my book goal and make it tangible I had to make it attractive and ensure it was something I wanted to achieve. Many of us make New Year resolutions – we need a fresh start, a clean break. We start with our resolutions and ...what happens? Often they fall by the wayside. Keep fit centres and gyms make their biggest killings from members who sign on with every good intention the day after the end of festivities and whose unrealistic, unplanned and impulsive good intentions have evaporated by the end of January. Easy pickings – just like taking candy from a plump, overweight toddler! Again, it boils down to this concept of focusing on what you WANT rather than upon what you don't want. That focus is key. The reason our New Year's resolutions tend to fall by the wayside is that we don't have structure to them, we don't put enough focus on them and we let life get in the way. Remember the heat-seeking missile – once we lock onto something, once we really go for something and set a deadline, that goal is invariably achieved. Within the brain there is a Reticular Activating System (RAS). The main function of this is to control our focus. Once you decide to treat yourself and buy a product such as a car or a new outfit you begin to notice things associated with those products everywhere. Every second car on the road seems to be the model you are looking at, and everyone else seems to be wearing the outfit you thought was unique.

Here's a powerful thought for the RAS....one thing we all have in common is a bank account of time. Our years all last the same length of time, and we have the same amount of weeks in our months, the same number of days in our weeks, hours in our days and minutes in our hours. Yet none of us (with the exception of a few) know how long we have actually got to live. We don't know whether it's days, months or years. Hopefully, it's years. But too many people go to their deathbed uttering words of regret, wishing they had loved more, given more, travelled more, given more back to this wonderful world that is ours. You don't often hear of people saying, as that moment of final truth approaches, that they wish they had bought a bigger car, worn designer labels or spent more time at the office. Instead, they will identify with the things that have real value and purpose in our world.

Purpose

And so – what is *your* purpose in this world today? Life is very, very short.

> *"It's not the hours that we put in that count; it's what we put into the hours."*
>
> (Anon)

SMARTER Goals

One of the best ways to think about goals is to focus on SMARTER goals. You need to make the goal very **S**pecific, make it **M**easurable, and it needs to be **A**greed; you need to tell important others of your goal. Then make it **R**ealistic and put a **T**imescale on it. **E**valuate the goal and **R**eview it, so the goal then becomes **SMARTER**.

Let's take an example. You decide you want to run a marathon. So – be **specific** about it. It's not the New York, or the Paris Marathon, it is the London Marathon. Make it even more specific than that and say which year you want to run it in. Is it 2007? 2008? Or 2009? Then make it *very* specific. What date is it? Is it the 17th, or the 18th of April? Be really, *really* specific about it. Is it 26 miles? No its not. It is 26.2 miles? We now know it is 17th April

ACTIVITY BOX

Read this to yourself and mentally tell your conscious mind to shut up allowing your subconscious to do the work

- Create an image or picture in your mind of when you brushed your teeth two weeks ago. Imagine where you were doing it, how you were doing it, what the colour of the toothbrush was, what it felt like and smelt like. Create a picture, and point to where that picture is.
- Now I would like you to think about brushing your teeth in two weeks time. I would like you to think about creating a picture, an image, a feeling. Point to where that picture is in the future.
- You will notice that the two images are in different areas. If you can imagine drawing a line from the past to the future and then pushing it way out in front of you or off to the side of you. This is your brain's way of working out the difference between your past and your future.
- Having pushed your time line out into the future, imagine yourself now in six months' time. Notice what you look like, sound like, how you feel, what the people around you are doing and how they look. Are you still in the same workplace? Are you still doing the same old things you have been doing for quite a while?
- Now look at yourself in one year's time. Go through that process again: see what you look like, examine how you'll feel, what the people around you are doing. Do you feel any different?
- Repeat the exercise moving three, five and ten years ahead. What is different?

Now I would like you to think about another line, your goal line.

- Think about all the short-term goals you want, the possessions and commodities you have desired. Think too about the achievements you have wanted for others, those close to you. These could be work goals, even promotions. Picture those goals being achieved and point to where that picture is.
- Then I would like you to think about your medium term goals, those travel goals, perhaps they are the sort of house you would like to live in, the sort of family that you would like to have, the relationships that you want to have with people. The friendships, the places that you want to go. Picture and feel these goals, noting where that picture is.

- Finally see the long-term goals, those same objectives of happiness, relationships and success ten years down the line. Picture these and point to where that picture appears. Draw an imaginary line between your short term and long term goals.

Now return to that first line, your time line, and compare its direction to your goal line. Point to where your time line goes with your RIGHT hand. With your LEFT hand, point to where your goal line goes. If they are going in very different directions your brain has not accepted that your goals are a feature of your future. If they are going parallel your brain has accepted your goals and you are a step closer to achieving them (seeing is believing).

Brilliant! Einstein would be proud of you. By doing this exercise you have just started to use both hemispheres of your brain to look into the future and visualise who you want to become and what you want to achieve.

2007. The goal is now defined. Your declared intention is to run the London Marathon of 26.2 miles on April 17th 2007.

The next step is to work out how you are going to **measure** your success. It would be madness to start training a week before the Marathon (as I did in 2005 and boy did it hurt!). You may need to give yourself a year. Set yourself a specific date a month from the start of your training on which you want to complete a five mile run. In the second month you could work up to running ten miles and then twelve miles in the third month and so on. The next step is to make it achievable and agree it with people. When doing this bear in mind that goals can be split into 'go up goals' and 'give up or take up goals':

- 'Go up goals' – You want to be careful who you share and agree these with. They are goals addressing an area of your life which you wish to improve. For example, getting a job promotion: if a colleague was also going for the same promotion then the last thing you want to do is share your goal with that person. They may attempt, if they can, to consciously or subconsciously sabotage your chances of success.

- 'Give up and take up goals' – These address something that you wish to give up, or take up. By sharing these with as many people as possible, telling them how you are going to do it, when you are going to do it and why you are going to do it, those you share it with can provide you with the support and encouragement you need to achieve your objective. The loss of face in front of them can also stop you backing out or losing resolution! As I found when writing my book.

After you have agreed with yourself that you will, indeed, run the London Marathon you need to make sure that the goal is realistic. Is it realistic that within just one year you can groom your body to run an amazing 26.2 miles? Maybe you need to take two years, or it may be very realistic to train for it in just six months. You need to make sure your goal is **realistic** and you do this by writing it down and checking it with others. Once you put a timescale on it and say when you are going to start and when you are going to achieve your goal, then it becomes very real. Start with the end goal in your mind, for this technique focuses the brain to work to a deadline.

To get from a SMART to a SMARTER goal evaluate and check your progress. In this case you could monitor success through a training chart to **evaluate** targets and see if you have reached the correct distance set for that month. You then need to **review** the results of the evaluation. If in the second month, you aimed to start running 10 miles, but are already achieving this, then you can review your targets and even raise your game. Goals need to be very malleable and flexible. But the bottom line is that you have got to have a deadline. That deadline is something you have to work to because the human brain needs a focus.

A very important factor in goal achievement is your <u>will</u> to achieve it. As we have discussed, your will to do anything can be measured on a scale of 0–10 with 10 being the absolute *"That must happen"*. It will happen, 100% definite. At the other extreme there is 0, *"Don't even want to start"*. If your will is less than five you are almost guaranteed to fail to achieve your goal.

After you have thought about how you are going to do it, think about giving it a numerical value. Do you fail to plan or plan to fail?

I have mentioned 3 times that it takes 21 days to change a habit. Think about the patterns that we lay down, those things that we do over and over again. If we can break the pattern, if we can break the chain for just 21 days, then it <u>will</u> make a difference. That is 21 days of doing something differently, of stopping doing something or starting to do something. As Nike say *'Just do it'*.

In order to hold that focus needed for goal achievement, avoid setting too many goals at once. One of the main reasons people fail to achieve their goals is that they get fed up with not being able to make it happen. Therefore, in the beginning, think about really small manageable goals, ones that you <u>know</u> you can achieve. Going for big goals such as being two stone lighter, giving up smoking, chocolate, and alcohol will often be too much all at once, and very boring! Moderation is a challenge, so if you find the concept hard, then cut from what harms you. Putting smoke, fat and excess poisons such as alcohol or caffeine into your amazing body will be short term gain for long term pain! If you can think about doing small things, and building them up slowly, you will empower yourself to achieve what you want. The journey of 1000 goals starts with achieving the first one and that step needs to take you in the <u>right</u> direction. Successfully achieving that first goal will help with the next one! Step by step.

ACTIVITY BOX

Fill in SMARTER for the first goal you have chosen

SPECIFIC: What is the specific goal you want to achieve?

MEASURED: How will you measure it? By time, performance, financial value?

AGREED: Who will you share this goal with? Who will provide you with the support you need?

REALISTIC: Is it realistic for you to achieve this within the measures you have set yourself?

TIMED: What is the time limit you have put on the goal? When will you achieve it by?

EVALUATE: How will you know you are on track?

REVIEW: How often will you review your progress?

Write them down; put them where you and others can see them on a daily basis at the forefront of your mind.

Good **L.U.C.K.** – Labour Under Correct Knowledge.

Act on your goal now for the past has gone, the now is the 'present': our greatest gift for tomorrow.

The word 'decision' means cut-from, really cut from what you did, to what you are going to do.

Keep your focus positive; believe in yourself as a 'human doing' not just a 'human being'. Give yourself and others the utmost respect.

Do:
- Bee SMARTER.
- Positively replace what you want with what you need.
- Begin with small goals.
- Decide on your beliefs.
- Focus on one goal at a time.

Remember:
The way you talk about a goal is important. Talk in terms of "I can, I will, do more."

Your Will needs to score greater than 5 out of 10 for your goal to be realistically achievable.

Success, success, success: Success by the inch is a cinch, but by the mile it can take a while.

Notes

Notes

CHAPTER SEVEN

Sting in Your Tail

(Motivation)

Pocket Rocket!

In a western world where we see many wanting more and giving less it is always refreshing to see a person who reverses this trend. I first met Philippa when I was working for John Ridgway.

I knew I would like Philippa before we even met, everyone talked fondly of her. True to their word she is an amazing individual. Sometimes referred to as a Pocket Rocket or Duracell Bunny, she is unstoppable, one of the most hardworking, selfless and caring people I have ever met. She is the person who would give you her last penny. Never once have I heard her comment on all she does for others. She just does it. Her motivation is constant.

Amidst working as an outdoor instructor she has been a National Hunt Jockey, and cycled 17,000 miles from Alaska to Rio de Janeiro for the World Wildlife fund helping people become aware of their environment. She runs a deer farm, continues to instruct in the outdoors, maintains a family, and still finds the time to climb and train towards her Mountain Instructor Award. Her continuous motivation and drive to achieve all this and still put time into herself, and mostly others, amazes and inspires me. I have worked with her on many courses and often find it hard to keep up!!

She is the ultimate human motivation machine. A joy to be around, her enthusiasm and energy is contagious. Spend time with her and your batteries are recharged!

We all have needs. Those needs go from total peak experiences where we sit and watch a sunrise or a sunset with someone we love, to the very basic life-survival needs for warmth, shelter and food. In addition, there is the need to be motivated. If we were not motivated to find food, to find love, or shelter to name but a few, then we would not be able to survive.

As human beings, or as I call them human doings, we are 96% similar to a pig or a horse (Alan Pease[13]). What stands us apart is our ability to think and use our minds to gain a higher level of motivation. The two main drivers in life are pain and gain. These opposites relate to everything we do. We can work out whether there is more pain, or more pleasure in each situation we encounter. People do things saying they don't want to do them, but the fact is that the pleasure of doing them is greater than the pain of inaction. We stop only when the pain becomes greater than the pleasure.

People can bumble along through life just going with the swarm. They bumble through work and bumble through their home life, moving constantly towards the bright, pretty flowers and not really questioning the direction they're taking. Until, that is, they hit one of life's windscreens! As the windscreen comes closer and closer they have to make a quick decision, whether to go left or right, up or down. But by then it is too late and the decision of avoidance is mere reaction without thought or planning.

What we need to think about is being...proactive. Fly out from the middle of the swarm and check where you are going, do your own navigation. Is it the direction you want to be going in? Should you find another swarm going a different way? Should you try going it alone? It is often only once we suddenly see the windscreen racing towards us that we begin to question our position. That windscreen could be a death in the family, being made redundant, or the break-up of a relationship. But by then it is often too late. Bee in a position where you can respond – to be 'response-able', 'able-to-respond' rather than simply react to a situation determined and imposed upon you by others.

Motivators

Unlike the horse and pig we are not only governed by our basic day to day existence. We are able to look ahead and create a compelling picture of the future that motivates and inspires. Therefore the majority of us are not just thinking about our next bit of food or shelter. When we respond to our world we are in control. We can plan for it, deal with it, and be flexible when it changes. As reactors we are controlled by our world, forced into situations made by others causing stress and 'learned helplessness' (Seligman 1965). To increase our control and responsiveness understanding where our motivation comes from is vital. The motivators are:-

1. **Internal** motivators – are all the things that make us feel good *inside*, the things that we do. Maybe it's charity work for others, doing a favour for a friend, or just seeing something through to a satisfactory conclusion. Whatever it is, it's that thing or activity that makes us feel proud and good about ourselves.
2. **External** motivators – are the *external* factors that make us feel good. Such as money, or our favourite outfit or what people do to us, or give to us.
3. **Towards** motivation – this is the way that we move towards something in a positive way due to the pleasure it brings. Think about how you got up this morning. If you had a 'towards' motivation you might be woken up by the opportunity clock, as Zig Ziglar[26] calls it, and think *'fantastic, a new day'*. You leap out of bed, thump your chest like Tarzan, stand there gargling cornflakes and you're filled with excitement, looking forward eagerly to what the new day will bring. One thing's for sure, you're on a roll. This day is going to be good.
4. **Away** from motivation – the motivation stems from the desire to get *away* from something or someone that creates pain for you. For example, the motivation to leave your job may be because you do not like your boss. If you have an 'away

from' motivation, then perhaps the alarm clock went off and you thought five more minutes in bed…five more minutes in bed…just five more. Eventually you got up simply because you wished to avoid the consequences of staying in bed. You were motivated as a result of inaction rather than action. Somehow, this sort of day doesn't have the same sort of ring to it. This day, you sense from the outset, is going to be a long haul. And most of it is going to be uphill.

We can all put ourselves in both camps. We often go from one to the other, but we all tend to have a predominant type of motivation. Some people are motivated by being told they can't, while others are motivated by being told they can. Which one are you predominantly?

Action

We need to work out which type of motivation affects other people as well as ourselves. A lot of us are very good at making excuses. But the most important thing is to *take action*. If you break the word motivation down it means **move-to-action**. The first step is absolutely crucial and this begins with a powerful belief. "You must believe to achieve." It is when you lose the belief, that you lose the motivation. Belief and motivation are twin-pillars. Without belief I doubt Ellen MacArthur would have left her moorings let alone continued injured, exhausted and behind schedule on her round the world sail.

Begin by visualising the end result – what will it *look* like? How will it *feel*? How will it *sound, taste* and *smell*, when I have actually done what I have set out to do? If we can really visualise, if we can really feel and hear the outcome, then our will to achieve it will be greater and the achievement itself will thus become real. Immerse yourself in these sensory experiences. Think about the language you use. It must focus on the words '*until*' and '*will*'. If you use the mantra, "*Until I do it, until I do it*", and "*I will do it, I will do it*", it is those words, those two powerful words combined, that mean your goal will be achieved. I mentioned smell. It is a very powerful motivator. In our fantastic on-board computer is a neuro-structure called the amygdala; <u>we</u> have two of them.

Put your thumbs in your ears and put your middle finger over your eyes allowing your index fingers to rest on your forehead. Yes you do look silly but there is a reason!

An inch into your head from where your index fingers lie are your amygdalas. An almond shaped structure seated in the emotional brain very close to your olfactory bulbs (smell senses). (You can take your hands down now!) Imagine a switch on each amygdala if the switch is backwards it triggers off receptor chemicals that cause you to feel negative, anxious, worried and frightened. If it is clicked forward it causes you to become motivated, happy, positive and excited.

How do we click it forward I hear you shout? I like your enthusiasm but hold your horses!

Let me first show you how to click it back. Go to the nearest bin (garbage can for you Americans), breathe in deeply through your nose. If there are old fish heads in there I imagine your head has gone back in the same way that when a horse is negative or frightened its ears go back (Jack Norris[27]).

To click it forward (for the horse, their ears will go forward) go and find whatever smell you enjoy the most. For me it's honeysuckle, fresh cut grass or burning wood on an open fire. If you are sitting on a bus reading this please explain to the man/woman in front what you are doing before you start sniffing their neck!!

Your amygdala is the gateway to your frontal lobes this is where the seat of our higher intelligence lies. When the amygdala is clicked forward we open the channels to this vast untapped potential. This explains the benefits of aromatherapy, and why 'the nose knows'. For more information on this look up the work of Dr Lingo[28].

As 'human *doings*' we need to <u>do</u> things. What is it you want in life? What are your goals on this, as far as we know, our one chance on earth?

ACTIVITY BOX

Fill in this motivation map and extend it to help your mind focus on what you need:

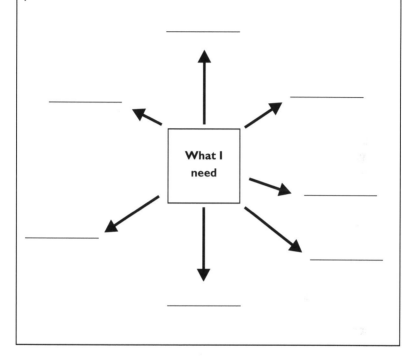

Bee Disciplined

Say with confidence what you are going to do and then stick with it. Tell yourself what it is that you want, and think about all the things that may be stopping you. There are forces driving us to get to where we want to be. But often, on that journey, we hit a block, a wall, that is like a force field. We need to be aware of that force field, for it is always there. It is the restraining forces on the other side keeping that wall in place that you need to climb over and look at.

They are the things that hold us back, the things that often stop us from doing what we want to do. Only by acknowledging all these forces can you work to remove and alter them. Once you can say what your restraining forces are, you can work them out clearly and start to move towards what it is that you want to achieve.

ACTIVITY BOX

Fill in both sides of the force field

What you are going to achieve	Factors that are stopping you

Amazing Fact Number Seventeen: It has been suggested, by scientists and psychologists, that in our society 95% of people will never achieve their ambition, never fulfil their true potential. The 5% left are those that actually go for it, and strive to reach that potential.

Which reminds me of fleas. Seriously! If you put some fleas in a test tube without a lid on – as you do – they will naturally jump up and out of the test tube. If you then take the same fleas and you put them into another test tube – but this time with a lid on the top – the fleas jump up and get a headache. Consequently they learn. They become trained and conditioned to jump just that little bit lower so they don't bang their heads. Now, take these same trained and conditioned fleas and put them in another test tube *without a lid on.* Those fleas will continue to jump to the same height as they did in the test tube with the lid in place.

This is how 95% of our nation, in my belief, behave. We think we can only jump so far or so high. We look at the 5% and think that only *they* can go higher and further, never us. We presume that somehow they are special. Yet, if you were to place a Bunsen burner beneath that test tube and apply heat, then those fleas would jump to great heights, believe me! This is what we need to do with 95% of our society who never attempt to jump beyond their own self-imposed ceiling. Metaphorically speaking only (of course!) we all need to have a Bunsen burner underneath us. We need to find our motivation; apply a little heat; stretch that comfort zone.

Support

Support is also very important in helping us to maintain that motivation to achieve our goals. If you have support, if you know other people are willing you to achieve your goal, then that gives you great motivational incentive. Remember the first chapter of this book? What did we say? We need to believe, above all, in ourselves. Once you have the belief that you can do something, very quickly people around you also believe that you can. That then becomes a constant cycle with people *willing* us towards our goal. The imperative starting point begins with a vision. We then need the impetus to start to think about achieving our goal. Once we begin to work toward our goal we become more confident – and once we start to feel more confident, we can then take the plunge and do what it is that we need to be doing. In my talks I demonstrate this by getting a member of the audience to break a piece of wood with their bare hands.

Having removed the forces that hold us back – all the fears of failure and under-achievement – we can move towards the things we need to achieve and take that plunge towards fulfilment. As a result of taking the plunge you will get a series of outcomes. Some people will call them failures, some will call them successes – but whatever you call them, all are outcomes, differences in the *status quo*, in that which was. You <u>will</u> get an end result. As a result of

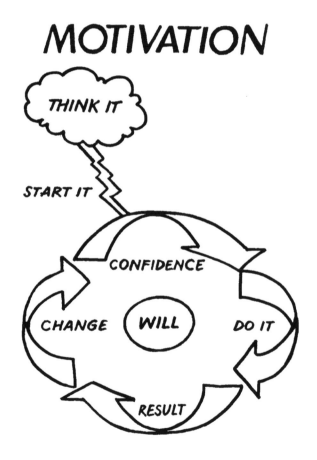

which you will notice that people around you will respond by giving you feed-back

Finally, it's all about you. Think, feel, visualise and create clarity. People say that seeing is believing. Visualise over and over again what it is you want to achieve. The more you do it the more you become it. (Landsberg 2005[30])

Do:
- Visualise what it is you want.
- Look at what motivates you.
- Bee self-disciplined.
- Understand how to motivate others.
- Recognise what it is that is holding you back.

Remember:
Support from others is vital to maintain motivation.

It starts and ends with you.

This is your life, your song.

Notes

Notes

Notes

Notes

The Bee All and End All

The Age of the Mind

Technology is doing two main things to us:

- We are becoming lazier.
- We are using our minds less.

This atrophy of mind and body is changing. The dawn of the Psychozoic age[6] is about to happen – an age where we will use the power of the mind to develop not just technology, but to make us happier and healthier. It will be a time to use our spatial, moral and humanistic energies to make the world a better place for future generations.

If we continue to live by the patterns of negative behaviour, attitudes and values, the future of this world, and our survival on it, is threatened.

When we can all work together to distribute wealth, resources, peace, love and kindness, we will not only survive, but will take a step closer to gaining an understanding of our true purpose on this beautiful planet.

The young will reap what we sow.

Remember and understand the control you have over the choices you make.

The Scouts have a great motto: 'Be Prepared'. To be prepared for opportunity in life is one way to broaden one's horizons. As Pen Hadow, an Arctic Explorer, once said to me – "Ships are safe in harbour but that's not where they are designed to be."

Deep into the Blue

We know not of the years, months, weeks, days or hours in
our lives.
We know of our own mortality, sure as the sun and moon will
rise and the seas will ebb and flow.
Of this, our first life, live it as a bright star.
Take time to find your compass, follow its needle, understand
that it will deviate.
Find love, peace and joy in you, to give to others.

Life can be turbulent as the wind
Amidst the blows of life, peace and beauty can be found in
people's spirit and the calmness of the land and sea.
Find it also in the wonder of a young child's eyes, and the
stillness of a crystal-clear river.

As water melts from the ice-capped mountains, it flows
furiously down hill like a small child.
The water cuts away the land forging its own new path.
The middle life of river is slower, deeper and wiser.
On reaching the sea fresh meets salt.
Surf blends the two as one to travel the world.

Follow your river, go with the flow.
Take risks, with each fork; to choose your path.
Set sail through life's seas.
Leave the estuary, its white sands and turquoise shallows.
Go deep into the blue.

Don't Tell The Bumble Bee

Look to the moon, sun, stars and heaven to plot your chart.
Strong winds will blow, waves will rise and lightning strike.
These are the things of life.
A new dawn will always rise, the seas will calm, sun will shine
    and the clouds will part.
Through adversity comes enlightenment to see God's beautiful
    world.

Anchor near dry land.
Take time to walk on white sand
To smell flowers
To hear nature
To see the beauty
To think deeply.

Jack Russell

References and Further Reading

1. **Magnan, A.** *Le Vol des Insectes* (1934)
2. **Miller, G.A.** *The magical number seven, plus or minus two.* Originally published in The Psychological Review, 1956, vol. 63, pp. 81–97
3. **Covey, S. R.** *The 7 Habits of Highly Effective People* Free Press; 15th Annv. Ed. (November 9, 2004)
4. **Black, J.** *Mindstore: The Ultimate Mental Fitness Programme* HarperCollins Pub. Ltd. (June 30, 1995)
5. **Balyi, Dr. I.** *"It takes 10 years of extensive training to excel in anything."* Herbert Simon, Nobel laureate Reprinted from Canadian Professional Coaches Association *Coaches Report*, Summer 2001, Vol. 8 No. 1
6. **Arntz, W. & Chasse, B.** *'What the Bleep do we Know'* (2004 DVD)
7. **Stone, Jack.** *Lego Super Hero...Can Do...Will Do...Done!*
8. **Potter, Prof. J.** *The Business of Leadership* with Alan Hooper Ashgate (1997)
9. **Mayer, Dr. W. E.** *How Full Is Your Bucket? : Positive Strategies for Work and Life* by Tom Rath and Donald O. Clifton Gallup Press Package edition (August 10, 2004)
10. **BBC health website** www.bbc.co.uk/health/ (January 2006)
11. **Pilzer, P. Z.** *The Wellness Revolution: How to Make a Fortune in the Next Trillion Dollar Industry.* John Wiley and Sons, New York. (2004)
12. **Mehrabian, A.** *Silent Messages: Implicit Communication of Emotions and Attitudes* Wadsworth Pub Co. 2nd ed. (June 1980)
13. **Pease, A. & Pease, B.** *Why Men Don't Listen and Women Can't Read Maps: How We're Different and What to Do About It* Broadway; 1st Broadway ed. (June 2001)
14. **Bandler, R. & Grindler, J.** *Using Your Brain-For a Change* by Richard Bandler Real People Pr. (May 1985)
15. **Turner, P. 'Bullet'** *Outdoor coach Black Catting* (1998)

16. **Huxley, A.** *The Doors of Perception and Heaven and Hell* Perennial Reissue ed. (July 1990)
17. **Goleman, D.** *Emotional Intelligence: Why It Can Matter More Than IQ* Bantam Reprint ed. (June 2, 1997)
18. **Gardner, H. & Goleman, D.** *Intelligence Reframed: Multiple Intelligences for the 21st Century* by Howard Gardner Basic Books (September 20, 2000)
19. **Bateson, G.** *Mind and Nature: A Necessary Unity* (1977) Bantam Press. New Ed Hampton Press (2002)
20. **Gandhi, M.** *The Mind of Mahatma Gandhi: My Hinduism Not Exclusive* (1926) Chapter IV. para 17.
21. **Vanier, J.** *Encountering 'the Other'* Veritas House (February 25, 2005)
22. **Frankl, V. E.** *Man's Search for Ultimate Meaning* Perseus Publishing (July 2000)
23. **Tuckman, B. W.** *Learning and Motivation Strategies* Prentice Hall 1st edition (July 10, 2001)
24. **Belbin, Dr. M.** *Team Roles at Work* Butterworth-Heinemann Reprint ed. (June 1993)
25. **Burka, J. & Yuen, L.** *Procrastination: Why you do it, What to do about it.* Re-issue ed. Addison Wesley (1990)
26. **Ziglar, Z.** *Goals: Setting and Achieving Them* Nightingale-Conant; Abridged ed. (August 1, 2002)
27. **Norris, J.** *'Thinking like a genius'* (2005)
28. **Lingo, T.D.A.** *'Brain in nature'* (1957)
29. **Buzan, T.** *Mind Maps at Work: How to Be the Best at Your Job and Still Have Time to Play.* Plume (November 29, 2005)
30. **Landsberg, M.** *The Toa Of Motivation: Inspire Yourself And Others* Profile Books; New ed. (March 30, 2005)
31. **Robbins, A.** *Unlimited Power Sound Ideas* Simon & Schuster Audio (February 1, 2000)

Thank you to all the above; your work, attitude and knowledge have inspired me.

Please contact us if we have not included you in this section

Jack Russell 2006

To Come...

© DTTBB children's book – a fun story of self belief, positive focus and confidence

© DTTBB DVD – "Put Buzz into Your Life and Bee Inspired"

© DTTBB – School manual 'Bee Positive' – a guide to support teachers coaching life skills in today's schools and education establishments.

© DTTBB website www.beepositive.co.uk

© DTTBB role model's and parent's book – a little handbook of 'do's' rather than 'don'ts'

For further courses, seminars, charity events, programmes and talks contact Jack:

0845 0652345

www.pdcinspiration.com